Merry
Christmas
Lois

The Inn Country Chefs Cookbook

Also from Berkshire House Publishers

The Inn Country USA Cookbook
C. Vincent Shortt

The Innkeepers Collection Cookbook
C. Vincent Shortt

Country Inns and Back Roads Cookbook
Linda Glick Conway

The Kripalu Cookbook: Gourmet Vegetarian Recipes
Atma Jo Ann Levitt

The Red Lion Inn Cookbook
Suzi Forbes Chase

Apple Orchard Cookbook
Janet M. Christensen and Betty Bergman Levin

Best Recipes of Berkshire Chefs
Miriam Jacobs

The Inn Country Chefs Cookbook

C. Vincent Shortt

Berkshire House Publishers
Lee, Massachusetts

The Inn Country Chefs Cookbook
Copyright © 1996 by Berkshire House Publishers

Front cover (from left to right): Cory Mattson, The Fearrington House; Lucy Hamilton, Richmond Hill Inn; C. Vincent Shortt; Craig Hartman, Clifton—The Country Inn. Photograph by Michael Cunningham.

"Inn Country USA" kitchen set design by Dr. Ann E. Shortt
Interior photographs by Craig Hammell and Michael Cunningham, except where noted.

Edited by Constance Lee Oxley
Cover design by Pamela Meier
Text design by Jane McWhorter
Production services by Ripinsky & Company

Library of Congress Cataloging-in-Publication Data
Shortt, C. Vincent, 1947-
The inn country chefs cookbook / C. Vincent Shortt.
     p. cm.
Includes index.
ISBN 0-936399-80-5
1. Cookery, American. 2. Hotels—United States. 3. Cooks—United States. I. Title.
TX715.S55885 1996
641.5973—dc20   96-15177

                                   CIP

ISBN 0-936399-80-5

10 9 8 7 6 5 4 3 2 1

This book is dedicated with respect, reverence, and love to the memory of my friend Jenny Fitch.

CONTENTS

NOTE

Recipes in each chapter are grouped by menu or type of food, following as closely as possible the sequence of presentations in the television series "Inn Country Chefs."

ACKNOWLEDGMENTS

Television programs and books are quite likely the least understood "team sports" in existence. Since I have had the good fortune of producing both as a part of the "Inn Country Chefs" public television series project, I feel a certain obligation to point out that producers cannot produce without scores of dedicated and talented people who share the vision and the goal, and authors cannot author without a similar team of hard-working people who embrace the same goal. In a very real sense, every person in the credit roll of our television programs is a co-producer. Similarly, every person involved in the development and creation of this cookbook is a co-author.

I am privileged to have had the co-production team at the University of North Carolina Center for Public Television as partners in the development, production, and distribution of this series. In particular, I would like to thank Tom Howe and Bob Royster for their willingness to share our vision and their foresight in assembling the talented team of players headed by Cindy Simoni, who made the production process happen. In addition, we owe a deep and sincere expression of gratitude to R.B. and the late Jenny Fitch, and to Executive Chef Cory Mattson, whose generous technical support put each chef at ease and whose encouragement enhanced the project at every turn.

This book and the series it accompanies would not have been possible without the tireless efforts of our line producer, Varian Brandon; our transcriber, Rosemary Stevens; and our project manager, Judy Emminizer. For her talented editorial input, her creative set design, her daily good counsel, and for putting up with me for the past 24 years, I would like to thank my wife, Ann.

And finally, I find myself thanking the usual cast of characters at Berkshire House Publishers in Lee, Massachusetts, who just keep on doing extraordinary things. To my publisher Jean Rousseau, whose unflagging dedication to tasteless bow ties has endeared him to both me and Mr. Blackwell forever, to my patient editors Constance L. Oxley and Philip Rich, and to dear Mary, the original prototype for the bumper car, I express my deep appreciation. It is an honor and a privilege to be associated with all of you.

C.V.S.

INTRODUCTION

Along the way to developing several hundred television programs and four books focusing on country inns and bed & breakfast's in the United States, we have made lifelong friends, tasted some of the best food in the land, and met some amazingly talented people. In the spring of 1995, I met with my friends and colleagues at the University of North Carolina Center for Public Television to talk about some of those talented people and to discuss an idea.

The idea was born out of the notion that as long as there have been televised cooking shows, there has been a debate about what makes them work best. We concluded that the strongest and the weakest link in recently created cooking shows has been the pervasive use of a single, on-camera "star." Based on the number of "special guests" that these shows bring into their programs, it would appear that they have made the same observations. Television audiences like variety in their programming, on their plates, and in their chefs!

From this observation, the concept for a studio-based cooking show was born. Our idea was to create a television series with not one, but *fourteen* different chefs. With a little creative scheduling, we could make it possible for the viewer to enjoy the series each week for more than three months and never see the same chef twice!

We selected fourteen regionally diverse chefs from some of the finest country inns and bed & breakfast's in the nation and assembled them, one at a time, over several weeks in the summer of 1995 in the studios of UNC-TV in Research Triangle Park, North Carolina. Each chef came prepared to create four different presentations for our cameras. When it was all said and done, we had fifty-six new and original "Inn Country Chefs" cooking shows to offer to public television audiences around the country.

In order to achieve some production efficiencies, we shot the programs on a rigorous, virtually nonstop daily schedule. Since each program required considerable advance preparation, each chef arrived in North Carolina a day or two prior to production day. A splendid country inn, The Fearrington House in Pittsboro, North Carolina, provided prep facilities, and their talented young chef, Cory Mattson, assisted each chef through the preparation procedures.

The set used for "Inn Country Chefs" was made possible through the generous support of series underwriter, Thomasville Furniture Industries, whose beautiful Terrace Garden Collection is featured in the "Inn Country Chefs" set. We would like to thank several, local North Carolina companies, such as Le Bleu Bottled Water, Whitney Decorating, and The Stocked Pot, whose generosity truly added so much to the overall production.

Each chef presented his or her recipes in several television programs, some devoted to menus, others devoted to particular types of foods—entrées, desserts, special presentations, and the like.

In this book we have included as many of these recipes as space allows, grouping them by menu or type of food, as indicated on the title page for each chapter.

To the fourteen featured chefs, I extend my heartfelt appreciation and congratulations for the role that each played in this unique collection of culinary treasures.

Chapter 1

Fruit & Cheese Display

Stuffed Snow Peas & Cherry Tomatoes

Creole Shrimp Cocktail

Artichoke Heart Strudel with Tomato Puree & Fresh Dill

*Pears Poached in Port Wine with
Crème Anglaise & Red Wine–Caramel Sauce*

Rose Inn Honey-Almond Duck

Ice Cream Pie with Red Wine–Caramel Sauce

Stuffed Portobello Mushrooms with Watercress Rémoulade

Stuffed Quail in Wild Grape Sauce

CHEF SHERRY ROSEMANN
Rose Inn, Ithaca, New York

COURTESY SHORTT STORIES PRODUCTIONS

Sherry Rosemann on the set of "Inn Country Chefs."

CHEF SHERRY ROSEMANN
Rose Inn, Ithaca, New York

It is one thing to dress for dinner, if you are dining. It is quite another matter altogether to dress for dinner, if you are cooking dinner. Meet Sherry Rosemann, one of the few innkeepers who likes to dress to the proverbial "nines," whether she is dining or serving. This Texas-born student of microbiology and social work in her preinnkeeper life came by her love of design quite naturally—by birth in fact. The daughter of a noted interior designer, Sherry's good taste and appreciation for design excellence shows everywhere in the Rose Inn. But nowhere in the inn is her attention to detail more appreciated than when she serves her guests on her elegant and beautiful china.

If there is such a thing as a match made in innkeepers' heaven, it surely must be this one. Charles Rosemann, Sherry's husband, is a Berlin-born and Black Forest-bred graduate of the Heidelberg Hotel College. He honed his considerable skills as a hotelier in Switzerland and the French Riviera before coming to the U.S. for stints with Hiatt, Sheraton, and eventually The Peabody in Memphis, Tennessee.

Dinner at the Rose Inn is more of a celebration than a meal. Wherever possible, Sherry and Charles surprise their guests with fresh-cut flowers from their garden—roses take center stage here—and with bright, edible pansies at every seating. The fruits that grow on the grounds provide more than ample opportunity for Charles to show off his canning skills with jams and preserves, which find their way into all manner of entrées and desserts.

Fruit & Cheese Display

Oranges

Apples

Large bunches grapes (3 colors)

1 large pineapple

2 pints fresh strawberries

2 large bunches bananas

2 cantaloupe, each crowned into 2 halves

Melon ball/blueberry mixture

2 kiwifruits, each crowned into 2 halves

Maraschino cherries (for center of each kiwifruit half)

Figs

Cherries

Plums

Peaches

4 to 5 different types favorite imported cheeses (hard cheeses cut into $3/4$-inch cubes and wedged soft cheeses)

Best-quality appetizer crackers

> You might be wondering what a *Fruit & Cheese Display* is doing in this upscale, elegant collection of fine inn recipes. Well, here is a surprise for you. When you see how Sherry orchestrates this recipe, you will understand. She is full of interesting little tidbits and hints on how this is accomplished, but one very important piece of advice is *elevation*. Elevation is the magic ingredient in creating a visually arresting and tantalizing array of fruits and cheeses that will have your guests asking, "How did you do that?"

Needed Items:

A large platter

A wire triangle, pyramid-shaped frame with open wired holes or a frame built with polystyrene, a knife to shape the pieces, and skewers to pin pieces together

Bamboo skewers and various lengths of brochette skewers

To make the fruit display: If the wire frame is used, fill the cupped holes with the oranges and apples to provide anchors for pinning the grapes and other fruit onto the frame. If the polystyrene form is used, then several small pineapples cut lengthwise can be skewered to the frame to cover.

Using the grapes in large bunches, start skewing the grapes to the frame to provide a background base, alternating with contrasting colors next to each other to provide definition. Anchor each piece securely so as the fruit builds up and cascades off the frame, it will be well balanced and stable.

Carefully cut the pineapple in half lengthwise through the top leaves, leaving the leaves attached to each half pineapple. With a sharp knife, hollow out the pineapple flesh and remove from the shell, reserving the shells as "boats." Remove the core from each half pineapple, cube the flesh, and fill the 2 shells with the cubes. Dot the top of each pineapple boat with the whole strawberries.

Cradle the bunches of bananas around the pyramid to provide support and to create angle and height for the pineapple boats. Angle the bananas toward the center, placing the pineapple boats atop the bananas. If necessary, secure the pineapples onto the center with skewers. Place the crowned melon halves on the center mass and anchor well into the center with skewers, then fill with the melon ball/blueberry mixture.

Once the large elements have been secured on the center structure, dot the display with the small pieces of fruit, such as the figs, cherries, plums, peaches, etc.

Arrange some of the larger fruit around the base of the pyramid and dot with more strawberries. Top the pyramid with a skewered kiwifruit crown and place the other kiwifruit crowns around the display.

To make the cheese display: On the large tray, make a pie-shaped arrangement of the soft cheeses with the points of the wedges pointing toward the center. Garnish each wedge with 1 strawberry sliced into a fan shape. Cascade the cubed cheese from the center and down the sides of the soft cheese wedges. Arrange the crackers around the outside rim of the platter. Serve.

YIELD: VARIABLE APPETIZER SERVINGS

Stuffed Snow Peas & Cherry Tomatoes

24 snow peas
2 tablespoons finely chopped fresh chives
Three 8-ounce packages cream cheese, at room temperature
1 pint cherry tomatoes, equally sized
3 to 3 ½ ounces (5 slices) smoked salmon
Red food coloring

Trim and string the snow peas. With a small, sharply pointed knife, start at one end of each pea and using the tip of the knife as a guide, cut the pea open along the side that does not contain the peas. Set aside.

In a food processor, place the chives and process until *very* finely chopped. Add two packages of the cream cheese and blend well. With a pastry bag fitted with a star tip, pipe the cream cheese mixture into the reserved snow peas and refrigerate the stuffed peas until firm.

Slice the tops off the tomatoes, seed, and turn upside down to drain on paper towels.

In the food processor, combine the remaining cream cheese, salmon, and 1 to 2 drops food coloring and process until smooth. With the pastry bag fitted with the star tip, pipe rosettes into each tomato and refrigerate the stuffed tomatoes until firm. Arrange the tomatoes in the center of a serving plate and surround with a fan of the peas. Serve immediately.

YIELD: VARIABLE APPETIZER SERVINGS

Creole Shrimp Cocktail

24 large fresh shrimp (20 to 32 count), peeled and deveined with tails
1 small red onion, very thinly sliced
1 lemon, very thinly sliced
One 8-ounce jar creole mustard (Zatarins)
1 cup olive oil
Fresh mixed greens, rinsed, dried, and shredded

In a large pot of boiling water, drop the shrimp and cook for 2 minutes, stirring constantly, or until the shrimp turn pink and are cooked through. (Shrimp should not be tightly curled or overcooked.) Drain in a strainer and place the shrimp on ice to stop cooking. When cold, pat the shrimp dry with paper towels and chill.

In a small bowl, combine the onion and lemon slices. Cover and chill. In another bowl, slowly whisk together the mustard and oil until very well blended. Chill for 20 to 25 minutes.

In a large bowl, combine the chilled shrimp, onion mixture, and mustard mixture and gently stir together, coating well. Drain and reserve the sauce. Set aside the coated shrimp.

Divide the reserved sauce among 8 very small cups. Place the cups in the center of small bowls and surround with the mixed greens. Arrange 3 shrimp in each small cup and serve immediately.

YIELD: 8 APPETIZER SERVINGS

Artichoke Heart Strudel with Tomato Puree & Fresh Dill

Two 14-ounce cans artichoke hearts (10 whole artichokes), chopped
$^1/_2$ cup mayonnaise
$^1/_2$ teaspoon garlic salt
1 egg, beaten
1 teaspoon Tabasco sauce
$^3/_4$ cup freshly grated Parmesan cheese
One 8-ounce package phyllo pastry, thawed
1 cup (2 sticks) margarine, melted
Dried bread crumbs
Aniseeds
1 recipe *Tomato Puree & Fresh Dill* (see recipe below)
Fresh dill, chopped

Tomato Puree & Fresh Dill

$^1/_2$ cup tomato puree
Garlic salt to taste
1 tablespoon chopped fresh dill
2 dashes Tabasco sauce or to taste

In a small bowl, mix together all of the ingredients until well blended.

In a medium-sized bowl, mix together the first six ingredients until well blended. Refrigerate until ready to use.

Place 1 sheet of pastry on a work surface and brush on the margarine to cover one half of the pastry. Sprinkle bread crumbs over the margarine half. Fold the unmargarine half over the margarine half and repeat the procedure.

Working with the shorter side towards you, place 1 heaping tablespoon of the chilled filling in the center at the end and roll away from you (two rolls). Then fold in both sides of the pastry towards the center. (This will keep the filling from running out.) Continue rolling until you get to the end, always placing the end of the pastry on the bottom.

Preheat oven to 350° F. Brush the pastry with more margarine and sprinkle the aniseeds over the top. Place on a baking sheet and bake for 15 minutes or until golden brown. Let cool slightly.

Place 1 tablespoon *Tomato Puree & Fresh Dill* on each plate. Cut the strudel and place each serving on the puree. Garnish with the dill and serve immediately.
YIELD: 8 TO 10 SERVINGS

It is a safe bet that Charles' German background is hard at work on this spectacular dish. Enjoy this combination of artichokes, tomato puree, and fresh dill!

Pears Poached in Port Wine with Crème Anglaise & Red Wine-Caramel Sauce

2 large pears (Bartlett or Comice)
3 cups ruby port wine
1 cup granulated sugar
1 cinnamon stick
2 anise stars
6 whole cloves
1 whole nutmeg

Grated peel of 1 lemon
1 recipe *Crème Anglaise* (see recipe below)
1 recipe *Red Wine-Caramel Sauce* (see recipe below)
Vanilla-flavored whipped cream
Crystallized ginger, finely chopped

Peel the pears, trimming the blossom end, but retaining the stem. In a 1-quart saucepan, combine the port, sugar, spices, and lemon zest and bring to a boil, stirring constantly, to dissolve the sugar. Add the pears and, if not completely covered with liquid, add enough water to cover. Reduce heat to simmer and poach the pears for 20 minutes, or until a tester pierces easily. Carefully remove the pears with a slotted spoon and place into a sterilized 1-quart canning jar. Boil the poaching liquid until reduced by half, about 2 cups. Strain the hot poaching liquid over the pears and refrigerate for at least 2 days.

Ladle $1/4$ cup *Crème Anglaise* onto each large dessert plate. Cut the pears in half lengthwise and using a melon scoop, remove the center seeds. With a sharp knife, starting at the blossom end of each half pear, make thin, regular slices lengthwise toward the stem end, making each half into a fan and keeping the stem end uncut so it holds the "fan" together. Fan each half outward with the stem ends together in the center of each plate. Drizzle the *Red Wine-Caramel Sauce* over the pears.

Top with a dollop of the whipped cream and sprinkle on the ginger. Serve immediately.
YIELD: 4 SERVINGS

Crème Anglaise

2 cups milk
1 teaspoon pure vanilla extract
4 egg yolks
3 tablespoons granulated sugar

In a medium-sized saucepan, heat the milk on medium-high heat just to boiling. In a medium-sized bowl, beat together the remaining ingredients with an electric mixer until begin to thicken. Add the hot milk very slowly on low speed.

Return the mixture to the saucepan and cook on low heat, stirring constantly, until begins to thicken. Remove from heat and set aside.

Red Wine-Caramel Sauce

2 cups granulated sugar
$^1/_2$ cup water
$^1/_2$ cup burgundy wine
1 cup heavy cream
2 tablespoons unsalted butter

In a large saucepan, combine the sugar, water, and wine and bring to a boil. Continue boiling without stirring until the sauce registers 300° F on a candy thermometer and is a deep caramel color.

Remove from heat. Carefully stir in the cream and butter and cook on low heat, stirring for 5 minutes. Let cool to room temperature and store in a glass jar in the refrigerator.

Rose Inn Honey-Almond Duck

One 4 $^1/_2$ - to 5-pound duck, excess skin, fat, neck, and giblets removed

Glaze:
$^1/_2$ cup honey
$^1/_4$ cup orange marmalade
$^1/_2$ cup sliced almonds
2 tablespoons Dijon mustard

Preheat oven to 250° F. Rinse out the cavity of the duck and place the duck breast-side up in a roasting pan just big enough to hold snugly. (Do not use a roasting rack.) Cook the duck for 5 to 6 hours. Drain off fat and let cool. Remove the backbone and rib cage, leaving only the leg and wing bones. Cut the duck into quarters and scrape off any bits of fat that still remain under the skin.

Increase the oven temperature to 475°. Place the duck pieces skin-side up in a lightly greased pan and cook for 8 to 10 minutes, or until the skin is crisp.

Reduce oven temperature to 450°. To make the glaze: In a small bowl, mix together all of the ingredients. Spoon the glaze on top of each piece of duck and cook for 6 to 10 minutes more until the almonds are toasted. Serve immediately.

YIELD: 4 SERVINGS

Ice Cream Pie with Red Wine-Caramel Sauce

One 12-ounce package flaked coconut
$^1/_2$ cup (1 stick) margarine, melted
$^1/_2$ gallon mocha chip ice cream
1 cup sliced toasted almonds
1 recipe *Red Wine-Caramel Sauce* (see recipe on page 19)
Vanilla-flavored whipped cream
Edible flowers

Preheat oven to 325° F. In a 8- to 10-inch pie pan, mix together the coconut and margarine until the coconut is thoroughly coated. Pat the mixture down firmly into the pan, creating a "pie crust." Bake on the lower rack of the oven for 20 to 25 minutes, or until the coconut is evenly browned. Let cool on a wire rack. Cover and freeze.

Remove the ice cream from the freezer and let soften for about 10 minutes. Generously fill the frozen coconut shell with the ice cream and cover the top with the almonds. Cover with plastic wrap and freeze.

Remove from the freezer 10 minutes before serving. Spoon 2 tablespoons *Red Wine-Caramel Sauce* over each serving. Add a dollop of the whipped cream and garnish with a flower. Serve immediately.

YIELD: 6 TO 8 SERVINGS

To toast almonds: Preheat oven to 350° F. In a small baking pan, place the almonds and bake for 5 to 7 minutes or until golden, stirring frequently.

Stuffed Portobello Mushrooms with Watercress Rémoulade

Four 4-inch fresh portobello
mushrooms, cleaned
1 recipe *Watercress Rémoulade* (see
recipe below)

Marinade:
1 cup olive oil
1/4 cup finely chopped garlic
1 teaspoon salt
1 teaspoon freshly ground black
pepper

Filling:
3 tablespoons chopped garlic
2 cups chopped onions
1/2 cup white wine
Juice of 1 lemon
1/2 cup dried bread crumbs
1 pound fresh crabmeat, cartilage
removed
1 3/4 teaspoons freshly ground black
pepper
2 tablespoons Cajun spices
1 tablespoon ground paprika
Salt to taste
Cayenne pepper to taste

Remove the stems of the mushrooms and finely chop. Set aside.

To make the marinade: In a small bowl, mix together all of the ingredients. Brush the tops and the bottoms of the mushrooms with the marinade. Let the mushrooms marinate at room temperature for 30 minutes. Set aside the remaining marinade.

Grill the mushrooms (beginning with the top side) for 3 to 5 minutes on each side, or until the centers are soft. Drain on paper towels and set aside.

To make the filling: In a medium-sized saucepan, heat the reserved marinade and sauté the reserved chopped mushroom stems, the garlic, and onions for 4 to 6 minutes, or until the onions are tender. Add the wine and lemon juice and simmer for 5 to 7 minutes. Stir in the bread crumbs, crabmeat, black pepper, Cajun spices, and paprika and mix well. Cover for 10 minutes. Add the salt and cayenne pepper.

Preheat oven to 375° F. Stuff the mushrooms with the filling. Place on a baking sheet and bake for 10 to 12 minutes.   Place 1 mushroom on each small plate and drizzle the *Watercress Rémoulade* over the top. Serve immediately.

YIELD: 4 APPETIZER SERVINGS

Watercress Rémoulade

2 egg yolks
1 tablespoon fresh lemon juice
1 teaspoon Dijon mustard
1 teaspoon capers
1 teaspoon chopped garlic
$1/2$ teaspoon Cajun spices
$1/2$ teaspoon ground paprika
1 cup corn or canola oil
$1/4$ cup finely chopped fresh watercress
Salt to taste
Cayenne pepper to taste

In a medium-sized bowl, mix together the first eight ingredients. Fold in the watercress and add the salt and cayenne pepper.

Stuffed Quail in Wild Grape Sauce

1 recipe *Veal Mousse* (see recipe below)
8 semiboneless quail
Salt and freshly ground black pepper
   to taste
4 tablespoons vegetable oil
1 recipe *Wild Grape Sauce* (see recipe below)

Season the quail with the salt and black pepper. Stuff each quail with 2 tablespoons of the *Veal Mousse* and truss together to close.

Preheat oven to 450° F. In a large cast-iron skillet, heat the oil to smoking and sear the stuffed quail until browned on breast side. Flip and bake, covered, in the skillet for 10 to 15 minutes.

Place 2 quail on each plate and brush generously with the *Wild Grape Sauce*. Serve immediately.

YIELD: 4 SERVINGS

Veal Mousse

8 ounces lean veal meat
2 eggs
1 cup heavy cream
2 tablespoons chopped fresh chives
Salt and freshly ground black pepper
   to taste

2 tablespoons butter
4 ounces chopped fresh mushrooms
2 shallots, chopped
1/2 cup coarsely chopped blanched
   skinless pistachio nuts

In a food processor, puree the veal and eggs until smooth. While the processor is running, drizzle in the cream until well blended. Add the chives, salt, and black pepper.

In a small skillet, melt the butter and sauté the mushrooms and shallots for 3 to 5 minutes or until tender. Add the mushroom mixture and pistachios to the veal mixture and blend well.

Wild Grape Sauce

$1/2$ cup white wine
$1/2$ cup wild grape juice or white grape juice
$1/2$ cup Triple Sec or Cointreau liqueur
$3/4$ cup beef stock
Cornstarch (optional)
Salt and freshly ground black pepper to taste

Deglaze the skillet with the wine, grape juice, and liqueur and reduce, stirring constantly, until glazed. Add the stock and reduce by one-fourth. Thicken with the cornstarch, if necessary, and adjust the seasonings. Keep warm.

Chapter 2

Cassoulette d'Escargots

Napoleons of Sea Scallops with Smoked Salmon & Chive Sauce

Salmon & Oyster Tartare

*Roast Loins of Lamb in Black Olive Crust
with Port Wine Sauce*

Soft-Shell Crabs with Lemon, Garlic & Basil

Tropical Fruit Gratin

Pineapple Fritters

CHEF JACQUES THIEBEULT
The Homestead Inn, Greenwich, Connecticut

COURTESY THE HOMESTEAD INN

CHEF JACQUES
THIEBEULT
The Homestead Inn,
Greenwich, Connecticut

Is it an inn with a fine restaurant? Or is it a fine restaurant with an inn? Inevitably when you come across an inn with that kind of identity crisis, it is a sure bet that there is a talented and multifaceted chef hard at work in the kitchen.

The Homestead Inn in Greenwich, Connecticut, enjoys the distinction of being the country inn closest to midtown Manhattan, and thanks to Chef Jacques Thiebeult, owners/innkeepers Nancy Smith and Lessie Davison find themselves constantly accepting accolades for both their inn and their restaurant.

Jacques' impeccable credentials date to 1963 when he began his career in Paris at the Restaurant Nicolas. After working his way into arguably the most prestigious kitchen in France, as the Private Chef to Georges Pompidou, then prime minister of France, Jacques decided to broaden his culinary expertise even further at École d'Hôtellerie in Lausanne, Switzerland.

In 1973, Chef Thiebeult journeyed to New York City and the kitchens of Le Bec Fin. Between 1974 and 1978, he added to the considerable reputations of both Le Cygne and the venerable Le Cirque in New York before joining The Homestead Inn as Executive Chef. Every stop along the way for this talented chef has added to the subtle and elegant skill with which he serves Homestead guests.

Cassoulette d'Escargots

1 tablespoon butter
24 canned snails, drained and well rinsed
5 ounces fresh chanterelle mushrooms
2 teaspoons chopped shallots
4 tablespoons *Garlic Butter* (see recipe below)
$1/2$ cup heavy cream
$1/2$ teaspoon Pernod liqueur (optional)
Fresh parsley, chopped

In a medium-sized skillet, melt the butter and sauté the snails, mushrooms, and shallots for 3 to 5 minutes. Add the *Garlic Butter* and stir until melted. Add the cream and liqueur and reduce by one-fourth.

Divide the mixture among 4 ramekins and sprinkle with the parsley. Serve immediately.

YIELD: 4 APPETIZER SERVINGS

Garlic Butter

4 cloves garlic, coarsely chopped
2 shallots, coarsely chopped
$1/2$ cup (1 stick) butter
3 tablespoons chopped fresh parsley
Salt and freshly ground white pepper to taste

In a food processor, finely chop the garlic and shallots. Add the remaining ingredients and process until well blended.

Napoleon of Sea Scallops with Smoked Salmon & Chive Sauce

6 fresh jumbo sea scallops, cartilage
   removed
6 slices smoked salmon, halved
1 recipe *Chive Sauce* (see recipe
   below)
8 egg whites, slightly beaten
$^1/_2$ loaf crustless white bread, finely
   crumbled
6 tablespoons butter
2 bunches fresh watercress
Salt and freshly ground black pepper
   to taste

Slice each scallop horizontally into 3
disks. Place 1 piece of the salmon between
the disks of each scallop and stack. Chill
the scallop/salmon stacks for 30 minutes.

Dip each chilled stack in the egg
whites and coat with the bread crumbs.
In a sauté pan, melt 4 tablespoons of the
butter and carefully sauté each stack until
golden brown. Remove and keep warm.

In the hot sauté pan, melt the remaining butter and wilt the watercress, stirring
in the salt and black pepper. Slice each
warm scallop/salmon stack into pieces.

Place the watercress in the center of
each plate. Surround with the scallop/
salmon pieces and the *Chive Sauce.* Serve
immediately.

YIELD: 2 APPETIZER SERVINGS

Chive Sauce

1 $^1/_4$ cups (2 $^1/_2$ sticks) butter, divided
2 shallots, chopped
24 white peppercorns
$^1/_2$ cup dry white wine
$^1/_2$ cup heavy cream
2 bunches fresh chives, chopped
Salt and freshly ground black pepper
   to taste

In a sauté pan, melt $^1/_4$ cup of the butter and sauté the shallots and peppercorns for 3 to 5 minutes. Add the wine
and reduce to almost dry. Add the cream
and reduce by half. Add the remaining
butter, a little at a time, whisking constantly until thick. Stir in the chives, salt,
and black pepper.

Salmon & Oyster Tartare

8 ounces fresh salmon fillet, coarsely chopped
12 fresh oysters (Belon, Pemiquid, or New England)
1 cup chopped fresh chives
Juice of 4 lemons
Salt and freshly ground black pepper to taste
1/2 cup plain yogurt
Salt and freshly ground black pepper to taste
2 lotus roots, peeled and thinly sliced*
2 heads fresh Boston lettuce, rinsed, dried, and julienned
Green flying fish roe*

In a medium-sized bowl, combine the salmon, oysters, and chives. Add the juice of 2 lemons, the salt, and black pepper and set aside.

In a small bowl, mix together the yogurt and the remaining lemon juice, the salt, and black pepper and set aside.

Preheat oven to 300° F. Place the lotus root slices in a nonstick baking pan and bake for 5 minutes or until crisp.

Put a round mold in the center of each plate and divide the lettuce among the molds. Divide the reserved salmon mixture on top of the lettuce. Remove each mold and drizzle the reserved yogurt mixture around the salmon. Place 1 to 2 tablespoons fish roe on top of the salmon and arrange 3 lotus root chips on top of the yogurt mixture. Serve immediately.

Items are available in gourmet foods stores and Asian markets.

YIELD: 4 APPETIZER SERVINGS

Just the name of this elegant appetizer seems to send the palate soaring. When Jacques prepared this exciting dish for our cameras, the finished plate looked more like a carefully sculpted work of art than an exotic seafood appetizer. Every experience in the chef's distinguished background seems to find its way to the plate in this splendid dish.

Roast Loins of Lamb in Black Olive Crust with Port Wine Sauce

1 recipe *Port Wine Sauce* (see recipe below)
1 cup finely chopped Niçoise olives
1 cup dried bread crumbs
$1/2$ cup (1 stick) butter, melted
Salt and freshly ground black pepper to taste
$1/4$ cup canola oil
4 Idaho potatoes, peeled and thinly sliced
Two 2- to 3-pound boneless loins of lamb, cleaned
Salt and freshly ground black pepper to taste
2 tablespoons butter

> In this recipe, the black olive crust is such a new and unusual creation, you will be using it exclusively with a variety of roast meat dishes. With the lamb, this crust is simply and completely divine.

In a medium-sized bowl, mix together the olives, bread crumbs, melted butter, salt, and black pepper. Set aside.

Preheat oven to 350° F. In a large ovenproof skillet, heat the oil until smoking. Cover the bottom of the skillet with the potato slices until $1/2$ inch thick. Brown the slices evenly on both sides. Place in the oven and bake for 7 minutes. Remove the potatoes and keep warm.

Season the lamb loins with the salt and black pepper. In a large, hot skillet, melt the 2 tablespoons butter and sauté the loins. Brown all over and cook for 7 to 10 minutes or until medium-rare. Place the cooked loins in the   reserved bread crumb mixture and coat evenly. Let stand for 5 minutes.

Divide the potatoes among the plates. Slice the lamb and place on top of the potatoes. Drizzle the *Port Wine Sauce* around the plate and serve immediately.

YIELD: 4 SERVINGS

Port Wine Sauce

6 ounces lamb bones, chopped
2 tablespoons butter
2 shallots, chopped
2 tablespoons all-purpose flour

2 sprigs fresh thyme
$^3/_4$ cup port wine
1 $^1/_4$ cups lamb or beef stock

Preheat oven to 400° F. In a baking pan, brown the lamb bones in the oven.

In a large saucepan, melt the butter and sauté the shallots on medium heat for 3 to 5 minutes or until tender. Add the flour and cook, stirring constantly, for 5 minutes.

Add the thyme sprigs, wine, and stock and reduce by half. Add the browned lamb bones and simmer for 15 minutes. Strain the mixture and set aside. Keep warm.

Soft-Shell Crabs with Lemon, Garlic & Basil

12 fresh soft-shell crabs, gills, tails, and air sacks removed
2 cups milk
2 cups all-purpose flour
1 $^1/_4$ cups butter
16 cloves garlic, finely chopped
Juice of 8 lemons
4 bunches fresh chives, finely chopped
$^1/_2$ cup shredded fresh basil
$^1/_2$ cup shredded fresh mint
Salt and freshly ground black pepper to taste

Place the crabs in the milk, then dredge in the flour. In a large skillet, melt 1 cup of the butter and sauté the crabs for 4 minutes on each side, or until both sides are golden brown. Keep warm.

In the same skillet, remove the old butter and melt the remaining fresh butter. Add the garlic and sauté for 3 to 5 minutes. Deglaze with the lemon juice. Stir in the chives, basil, mint, salt, and black pepper and mix well.

Place 3 crabs on each plate and ladle the sauce over the crabs. Serve immediately.

YIELD: 4 SERVINGS

Tropical Fruit Gratin

8 egg yolks
1 1/2 cups granulated sugar
1/2 cup passion fruit liqueur (Alize)
1/2 cup fresh coconut milk
1 papaya, cut into 1/2-inch squares
1 mango, cut into 1/2-inch squares
1 kiwifruit, cut into 1/2-inch squares

1 passion fruit, cut into 1/2-inch
   squares
1/2 fresh pineapple, cut into 1/2-inch
   squares
1 banana, cut into 1/2-inch squares
1 guava, cut into 1/2-inch squares

In the top of a large double boiler over simmering water, whip together the egg yolks, sugar, liqueur, and coconut milk until reach the consistency of stiff peaks.

Place all of the fruit into an ovenproof, deep baking dish and spoon the egg yolk mixture over the fruit. Place under the broiler until golden brown. Serve immediately.

YIELD: 4 TO 6 SERVINGS

Pineapple Fritters

1 cup all-purpose flour
2 tablespoons granulated sugar
Pinch salt
1 1/2 cups milk
4 eggs, beaten
Pure vanilla extract to taste
1/4 cup (1/2 stick) melted butter

1 cup canola oil
1/2 fresh pineapple, peeled, cored, and
   sliced into rings
Flour
Granulated sugar
Confectioners' sugar
Coconut sherbet

In a small bowl, combine the 1 cup flour, the 2 tablespoons granulated sugar, and salt. In a large bowl, mix together the milk, eggs, and vanilla. Add the flour mixture to the egg mixture and mix together well. Stir in the butter.

In a large, deep skillet, heat the oil until very hot. Dredge the pineapple rings in 1 part flour and 1 part granulated sugar. Dip the pineapple rings in the batter and fry in the hot oil until golden brown. Drain on paper towels.

Dust with the confectioners' sugar and serve immediately with the sherbet.

YIELD: 4 SERVINGS

Chapter 3

Mesclun Salad with Fresh Basil Vinaigrette & Nightingale Nests

Scallops Botticelli

Herbed Rice in Zucchini Ribbon

Iced Granny Apple

Wine Broth

Salad Bouquet

Polenta-Crusted Game Hens

Seared Scallops with American Caviars

Heirloom "One-Bite" Butter Biscuits

National Soup of the Islands of Madeira

Edwardian Crème

CHEF DEEDY MARBLE
The Governor's Inn, Ludlow, Vermont

Chef Deedy Marble with husband Charlie.

CHEF DEEDY MARBLE
The Governor's Inn, Ludlow, Vermont

There is a little Four-Star Victorian inn at the foot of Vermont's Okemo Mountain where collections of knife rests, tea sets, and chocolate servers bespeak the whimsy and good taste of the innkeepers, Charlie and Deedy Marble. This is the lady who is widely credited with putting the entire innkeeping industry on the Australian map.

On her way to collecting virtually every honor available to innkeepers, from Vermont's Best Apple Pie to the winner of the *Yankee* Magazine Cook-Off, Deedy managed to get a likeness of her little inn on the back of more than 50-million Uncle Ben's Country Inn Rice boxes as part of the Country Inn Rice promotion. The Marbles have both spent time keeping their culinary skills finely tuned with time spent on both sides of the podium as students and teachers.

To give just a hint of the dedication of this pair of innkeepers, our production crew was pleasantly surprised to walk into The Governor's Inn kitchen and to be greeted by freshly baked breads. These innkeepers also had taken the initiative to retain the services of a food stylist to arrange their kitchen for our cameras. This kind of dedication to excellence and attention to detail is apparent in every dish prepared by Deedy for the "Inn Country Chefs" series.

Mesclun Salad with Fresh Basil Vinaigrette & Nightingale Nests

4 generous cups rinsed and dried
  mixed fresh greens
1 recipe *Fresh Basil Vinaigrette* (see
  recipe below)
1 recipe *Nightingale Nests* (see recipe
  below)

In a large bowl, toss the mixed greens with ¹/₂ to ³/₄ cup *Fresh Basil Vinaigrette.*

Divide the dressed greens among the salad plates and bank 3 *Nightingale Nests* against each serving of the greens. Serve immediately.

YIELD: 4 SERVINGS

Fresh Basil Vinaigrette

1 cup vegetable oil
¹/₂ cup extra-virgin olive oil
¹/₂ cup champagne vinegar
2 shallots, finely chopped
2 cloves garlic, finely chopped
¹/₂ cup chopped fresh basil
Salt and freshly ground white pepper
  to taste

In a blender or food processor, blend together all of the ingredients until well blended and smooth.

Get your knitting needles out for this one. The accompanying *Nightingale Nests* look daunting at first glance, but you'll find yourself leaving the knitting needle in the kitchen gadget drawer once you get the hang of preparing this tasty recipe.

Nightingale Nests

One 8-ounce package phyllo pastry,
  thawed
Melted butter
6 ounces goat cheese

Cut 12 sheets of the pastry 2 to 3 inches shorter than the length of #10 knitting needle. Lay 1 sheet on a work surface and brush lightly with the melted butter. Loosely roll the pastry around the knitting needle, leaving 2 to 3 inches un-rolled. Push the sides of the pastry toward the center of the needle, then remove the needle. Connect the edges of the pastry, creating a ruffled circle with the unrolled portion in the center forming a "nest." Repeat this procedure with the remaining sheets.

Preheat oven to 375° F. Fill the center of each nest with 1 tablespoon of the cheese and bake for 15 to 18 minutes, or until the pastry is browned and the cheese is slightly melted.

Scallops Botticelli

3 tablespoons olive oil
2 shallots, finely chopped
1 clove garlic, crushed with pinch salt
1 medium zucchini, julienned
$^1/_2$ medium red bell pepper, seeded, deveined, and julienned
Pinch cayenne pepper
Salt and freshly ground black pepper to taste
12 scallop shells
1 pound fresh bay scallops, rinsed and drained
6 teaspoons unsalted butter
2 tablespoons chopped fresh chives
2 sheets phyllo pastry, thawed
1 egg, lightly beaten
2 cups cooked white rice
Fresh mixed herbs, chopped
6 lemon slices

In a medium-sized skillet, heat the oil and sauté the shallots and garlic on medium heat for 1 minute, stirring gently. Add the zucchini and bell pepper and sauté the vegetables until just barely tender. Stir in the cayenne pepper and toss to blend. Remove from heat and season with the salt and black pepper. Let cool.

Divide the vegetable mixture among 6 of the scallop shells. Place 4 to 6 scallops on the shells and top each shell with 1 teaspoon of butter and a sprinkle of the chives. Cover with the remaining shells.

Preheat oven to 350° F. Cut the pastry into 1- or 1 $^1/_2$-inch-wide strips. Place the strips around the shell pairs to seal. Brush the pastry with the beaten egg. Place the pastry shells on a baking sheet and bake for 15 minutes.

Toss the rice with the herbs and place a mound of the rice on each plate. Place 1 pastry shell on the rice and garnish with the lemon slices. Serve immediately.

YIELD: 6 SERVINGS

Herbed Rice in Zucchini Ribbon

1 tablespoon olive oil
$^1/_2$ small onion, diced
1 clove garlic, finely chopped
1 stalk celery, finely diced
$^1/_2$ tablespoon tomato paste
1 cup uncooked white rice
2 cups chicken stock
1 bay leaf
1 sprig fresh thyme
$^1/_2$ cup chopped mixed fresh herbs (basil, marjoram, chives)
3 large zucchini, unpeeled
3 tablespoons butter

(This recipe requires one 20-inch piece PVC pipe, 3 $^1/_4$ inches in diameter, cut into 8 pieces, 2 $^1/_2$ inches long. PVC pipe can be purchased at any local hardware store.)

In a large skillet, heat the oil and gently sauté the onion, garlic, and celery until aroma develops in oil. Add the tomato paste and cook for about 1 minute. Stir in the rice and sauté for 2 to 3 minutes. Add the stock, bay leaf, and thyme and bring to a slow boil. Reduce heat to simmer, cover, and cook for 15 to 20 minutes, or until the stock is absorbed. Stir in the herbs just before serving.

While the rice is cooking, with a mandoline or sharp knife, cut the zucchini into several long strips. In another skillet, melt the butter and cook the strips until just wilted. Remove the strips to a work surface.

Place one piece of the pipe on each plate and line each piece with a single layer of the zucchini strips. Fill each piece with the hot herbed rice. Working quickly, remove each piece of pipe and serve the rice ribbons immediately.

YIELD: 8 SERVINGS

Iced Granny Apple

1 cup unsweetened applesauce
1 teaspoon ground cinnamon
1 cup fresh orange juice
2 tablespoons fresh lemon juice
1 tablespoon pure vanilla extract
1 cup heavy cream
Whipped cream
4 cinnamon sticks
4 large fresh strawberries, rinsed
Ground nutmeg

In a medium-sized bowl, mix together the applesauce and ground cinnamon. Stir in both juices and place the mixture in a food processor. While the processor is running, add the vanilla and slowly blend in the cream.

Divide the mixture into 4 small dishes and garnish each with a very small dollop of the whipped cream. Place 1 cinnamon stick and 1 strawberry on each side of the whipped cream and sprinkle with the nutmeg. Serve immediately.

YIELD: 4 SERVINGS

Wine Broth

1 medium apple, unpeeled and coarsely chopped
1 medium carrot, coarsely chopped
1 medium onion, coarsely chopped
1 cup canned stewed tomatoes
1 cup V-8 juice
$^1/_4$ cup beef stock, or 6 beef bouillon cubes
One (750 ml) bottle cabernet sauvignon or red wine of choice
One (750 ml) bottle sauvignon blanc or white wine of choice
1 teaspoon freshly ground black pepper
Fresh parsley, chopped
6 to 8 lemon slices

In a food processor, combine the apple, carrot, and onion and process until reach a coarse puree. Add the tomatoes, V-8 juice, and stock and blend together.

In a large pot, combine the tomato mixture with both wines and the black pepper and bring to a boil. Cover and cook at a rolling boil for at least 15 minutes. Strain the mixture through a fine strainer. Return the strained mixture to a clean pot and reheat.

Serve hot ($^1/_2$ cup per serving) in brandy snifters. Garnish each serving with the parsley and 1 lemon slice. (The broth can be stored in a glass container in the refrigerator for 6 to 8 months.)

YIELD: 6 TO 8 SERVINGS

Salad Bouquet

4 large tomatoes
4 leaves fresh red leaf lettuce, rinsed and dried
4 leaves fresh radicchio, rinsed and dried
4 scallions, rinsed and ends trimmed
4 pansies or other edible flowers
4 fresh asparagus spears, blanched
16 to 20 fresh enoki mushrooms, rinsed, dried, and trimmed
1/2 cup favorite salad dressing
8 cucumber rounds

Using a melon ball scoop, cut into each tomato at the stem end and carefully remove all of the seeds and pulp. Cut a leveling slice at the bottom of each tomato so the tomato sits level on a plate.

Place 1 leaf of the red leaf lettuce flat on a work surface and place 1 leaf of the radicchio directly on top. Place 1 each of all of the remaining ingredients (except use 4 to 5 mushrooms per serving) on top and roll up tightly. Repeat with remaining ingredients.

Using scissors, snip off the bottom of each "bouquet" even with the scallion and place in the center of each tomato. Open slightly to display all of the greens.

Spoon 2 tablespoons dressing in the center of each salad plate and place 1 tomato in the center. Arrange 2 cucumber rounds in the dressing and serve immediately.

YIELD: 4 SERVINGS

Polenta-Crusted Game Hens

Six 16- to 18-ounce game hens, washed, trimmed, and patted dry
3 small lemons, halved
$^1/_2$ cup (1 stick) unsalted butter
2 large cloves garlic, finely chopped
2 tablespoons chopped fresh rosemary
Good-quality cornmeal
Salt and freshly ground black pepper to taste

Spray a baking sheet with cooking spray, then cover with aluminum foil and spray again. Place 1 lemon half in the cavity of each hen. Tuck the wings under and tie the legs together.

Preheat oven to 425° F. In a small saucepan, melt the butter with the garlic and rosemary. Brush the hens liberally with the butter mixture, distributing the garlic and rosemary evenly over the hens. Sprinkle each hen with the cornmeal, salt, and black pepper.

Place the hens on the prepared baking sheet and bake for 10 minutes. Reduce temperature to 375° and bake for 45 to 60 minutes or until cooked through. Serve immediately.

YIELD: 6 SERVINGS

Seared Scallops with American Caviars

Clarified butter (see box on page 83)
18 large fresh sea scallops
18 to 20 large leaves fresh spinach, trimmed and blanched
1/2 cup homemade fish stock or bottled clam juice
Salt and freshly ground black pepper to taste
1 recipe *Brown Butter-Tarragon Vinaigrette* (see recipe below)
9 ounces salmon roe
9 ounces black American caviar
9 ounces whitefish caviar
Edible flowers

Butter a 9 x 13-inch piece of parchment paper and set aside. In a nonstick sauté pan, heat a thin film of the butter. When the butter is hot, add a few scallops at a time (do not crowd) and sear quickly on both sides. Repeat with remaining scallops. Remove the scallops to a rack placed on top of a sheet pan and carefully wrap each scallop in 1 spinach leaf, bringing the edges together on the bottom.

Preheat oven to 350° F. Place the wrapped scallops in a 9 x 13-inch baking pan with the stock. Cover with the prepared parchment paper and bake for 5 to 7 minutes or until firm to the touch.

Place 3 wrapped scallops on each plate. Drizzle with the *Brown Butter-Tarragon Vinaigrette* and top with 1 teaspoon of *each* caviar. Garnish with the flowers and serve immediately.

YIELD: 6 SERVINGS

> Here is an idea for adding zip to seared sea scallops that stirs the patriotic soul of even the most seasoned gourmand. This recipe is one of those that ends up tasting just as exciting as it sounds on paper. Have Fun!

Brown Butter–Tarragon Vinaigrette

$^3/_4$ cup unsalted butter

1 tablespoon extra-virgin olive oil

1 tablespoon softened unsalted butter

$^1/_4$ cup balsamic vinegar

1 shallot, finely chopped

1 clove garlic, finely chopped

Fresh tarragon, finely chopped

Salt and freshly ground black pepper
  to taste

In a small saucepan, melt the $^3/_4$ cup butter on medium heat and cook for 3 to 4 minutes, or until the solids separate and fall to the bottom, and the butter turns a nutty brown color.

Remove from heat and let stand for a few minutes. Skim off the solids and slowly pour off the clarified butter. Discard the solids on the bottom.

In another saucepan, reheat the clarified butter. Place the oil and the 1 tablespoon butter in a blender. With the blender running, add the heated clarified butter, the vinegar, shallot, garlic, tarragon, salt, and black pepper and blend together well.

Heirloom "One-Bite" Butter Biscuits

4 $^1/_2$ cups self-rising flour

2 sticks unsalted butter, cut into
  16 pieces and frozen

2 tablespoons sour cream

2 cups light cream or half-and-half

1 cup (2 sticks) unsalted butter,
  melted

1 cup granulated sugar

2 teaspoons ground cinnamon

1 teaspoon ground nutmeg

Spray 3 minimuffin pans (1 $^3/_4$ inch) with cooking spray.

In a food processor, place the flour on the bottom of the bowl and the frozen butter pieces on top. Pulse the flour and butter 12 times. Add the sour cream and light cream and pulse 6 times more, keeping the butter in little pea-sized pieces.

Preheat oven to 400° F. With floured hands, quickly roll the sticky dough into walnut-sized balls. Place the balls into the prepared muffin pans and bake for 11 to 12 minutes.

Remove the biscuits and roll half of the batch in the melted butter, then roll in $^1/_2$ cup of the sugar. Add the cinnamon and nutmeg to the remaining sugar and roll the remaining biscuits in the cinnamon mixture. Serve.

YIELD: 24 MINIBISCUITS

National Soup of The Islands of Madeira

¹/₄ cup (¹/₂ stick) unsalted butter
4 cups sliced white onions (Vidalia
  in season)
4 cups good-quality chicken stock

2 cups coarsely chopped fresh tomatoes
  or canned stewed tomatoes
1 cup Madeira wine
4 to 6 eggs, *lightly* poached and
  trimmed

In a large pot, melt the butter, then add the onions. Cover and cook until the onions are caramelized. When nicely yellowed, add the stock and tomatoes and simmer for 20 minutes.

Just before serving, stir in the wine. Place 1 poached egg in the bottom of each rimmed soup plate and ladle ³/₄ cup hot soup over the egg. Serve immediately.

YIELD: 4 TO 6 SERVINGS

Edwardian Crème

¹/₂ cup (1 stick) unsalted butter, at
  room temperature
4 ounces cream cheese, at room
  temperature
³/₄ cup confectioners' sugar

1 tablespoon fresh lemon juice
1 teaspoon pure vanilla extract
¹/₂ cup raisins
Fresh spearmint leaves, rinsed

Puree:
One 10-ounce package frozen unsweetened raspberries, thawed

In a medium-sized bowl, beat together the butter and cream cheese with an electric mixer until soft and light. In a small bowl, combine the sugar, lemon juice, and vanilla. Add the sugar mixture to the butter mixture and beat with an electric mixer on low until well blended. Fold in the raisins. To make the puree: In a blender or food processor, process the raspberries until smooth. Strain to remove seeds.

Place 2 tablespoons puree in the bottom of each glass dessert dish. With an ice-cream scoop, place a round ball of the crème on top of the puree. Garnish with a spearmint leaf and serve immediately.

YIELD: 6 SERVINGS

Chapter 4

Chilled Honeydew-Mint Soup

*Grilled Brochettes of Marinated Pork Tenderloin
with Summer Squash & Portobello Mushrooms*

Chocolate-Dipped Strawberries

Braised Salmon Fillets with Tarragon Velouté

*Bibb Lettuce Salad with
Dijon Mustard & Champagne Vinaigrette*

Ratatouille

Bailey's Irish Cream Cheese Torte

Butternut Squash Soup

Pan-Seared Tournedos of Bison with Cabernet Sauvignon Sauce

Chocolate Mousse Terrine with Raspberry Coulis

Crab Mousse Roulade & Cucumber Slices with Dill Butter

Fresh Fruit Tart with Mascarpone Cream

CHEF MICHAEL SHEEHAN
Prospect Hill Plantation Inn, Trevilians, Virginia

COURTESY PROSPECT HILL PLANTATION INN

*Chef Michael Sheehan
with father Bill Sheehan.*

MICHAEL SHEEHAN
Prospect Hill Plantation Inn, Trevilians, Virginia

Michael Sheehan wasn't born with a silver spoon in his mouth. But, truth be known, Michael probably was born knowing on which side of the dinner plate to set the spoon. With the French appreciation for food and wine contributed by his mother's side of the family and the Irish-American lust for life on his father's side, Michael began developing an appreciation for the celebratory side of food early in life. When he was 15, his family acquired and began operating Prospect Hill, the 1732 inn located in the Piedmont region of Virginia, near Charlottesville.

Upon graduation from college, Michael was able to spend his summers working in the Principality of Monaco on the French Riviera in the kitchen and dining room of Salle Empire at the Hotel de Paris. He also gained an early appreciation for the role of fresh fruits and herbs in fine cuisine while working in the market in Beausoleil, delivering the best available fresh produce to the diverse and discriminating restaurants and hotels of the Côte d'Azur.

The healthy contrasts of heritage, geography, upbringing, and style end up being interpreted throughout the luxurious surroundings of Prospect Hill.

Chilled Honeydew-Mint Soup

2 large honeydew melons, peeled and coarsely chopped
$^1/_2$ cup chopped fresh mint
$^1/_3$ cup chardonnay wine
Juice of 1 lemon
Granulated sugar to taste
6 to 8 fresh mint leaves, rinsed

In a blender or food processor, blend together the melon pieces, the mint, wine, and lemon juice, slowly adding the sugar, until the mixture is very smooth. Thin with water, if desired. Chill for 30 minutes.

Garnish each serving with 1 mint leaf and serve chilled.

YIELD: 6 TO 8 SERVINGS

The notion of a chilled soup says quite a lot about the sophisticated tastes both in the kitchen and in the dining room of Prospect Hill. The addition of fresh mint perks up the bouquet of this particularly refreshing summer soup.

Grilled Brochettes of Marinated Pork Tenderloin with Summer Squash & Portobello Mushrooms

Two 1-pound 8-ounce whole pork tenderloins, well trimmed
Salt and freshly ground black pepper to taste
2 fresh portobello mushrooms, trimmed and cut into 1-inch thick slices
2 medium yellow summer squash, cut into 1-inch thick slices
Hot cooked white rice

Marinade:
2 tablespoons crushed garlic
$1/2$ cup chopped onions
$1/4$ cup soy sauce
$3/4$ cup sesame oil
1 dried ancho chili pepper, chopped
2 tablespoons chopped fresh gingerroot
$1/4$ cup dry white wine
Juice of $1/2$ lemon

Cut the tenderloins into 1 $1/2$-inch thick medallions and lightly season with the salt and black pepper. Alternate the meat and vegetables on metal skewers and place the filled skewers in a shallow baking pan.

To make the marinade: In a medium-sized bowl, whisk together all of the ingredients until well blended.

Baste the skewered meat and vegetables with the marinade and let stand for 30 to 60 minutes, frequently coating with more marinade.

Place the skewers over a hot grill, turning once and brushing with the remaining marinade, and cook for 10 to 12 minutes, or until the vegetables are tender and the meat is firm to the touch.

Divide the rice among the plates and place 2 to 3 skewers on top of each serving of rice. Serve immediately.

YIELD: 4 SERVINGS

Chocolate-Dipped Strawberries

1 recipe *Dark Chocolate Ganache* (see recipe below)
2 pints large fresh strawberries, rinsed and not hulled

Cover a baking sheet with wax paper and set aside.

In the top of a double boiler over simmering water, slowly melt the *Dark Chocolate Ganache,* stirring frequently. Remove from heat. Dip the strawberries (green top up) into the chocolate to ¹/₂ inch below top. Dip again.

Place the dipped strawberries on their sides on the prepared baking sheet and chill for 1 hour or until firm. Peel the strawberries off the wax paper, one at a time, and serve chilled.

YIELD: VARIABLE SERVINGS

Dark Chocolate Ganache

8 ounces Callebaut dark chocolate (or best quality available)
³/₄ cup heavy cream
Dash favorite liqueur

In the top of a double boiler over simmering water, slowly melt the chocolate. When very soft, stir in the cream and liqueur. Immediately remove from heat. Chill and reheat as needed.

Braised Salmon Fillets with Tarragon Velouté

1 recipe *Tarragon Velouté* (see recipe below)
$^1/_4$ cup fish stock or clam juice
$^1/_4$ cup dry vermouth or white wine
4 slices onion, separated into rings
Four 6-ounce skinless salmon fillets
2 cloves garlic, finely chopped
$^1/_2$ stick butter, cut into thin slices

Preheat oven to 375° F. In a shallow-sided roasting pan, mix together the stock and vermouth. Scatter the onion rings in a layer on the bottom of the pan. Place the fillets on the bed of onion rings, sprinkle the garlic evenly over the fillets, and cover with the butter. Place the pan on the middle rack in the oven and bake for 10 to 15 minutes, or until the fillets are just firm and starting to flake.

Place 1 fillet on each plate and top with $^1/_4$ cup *Tarragon Velouté*. Serve immediately.

YIELD: 4 SERVINGS

Tarragon Velouté

1 teaspoon butter
1 tablespoon finely chopped garlic
1 tablespoon chopped roasted shallots
4 cups chicken consommé
1 cup white wine
$^1/_4$ cup cornstarch mixed with $^1/_4$ to $^1/_2$ cup water
4 cups cream
$^1/_2$ cup chopped fresh tarragon
Freshly ground white pepper to taste
$^1/_4$ cup clam juice or fish cooking juices

In a large pot, melt the butter and sauté the garlic and shallots for 3 to 5 minutes. Add the consommé and bring to a boil. Reduce heat to simmer. Strain off solids and return the mixture to the pot.

Add the wine and simmer for 15 minutes. Stir in the cornstarch mixture to thicken. Mix in the cream, tarragon, white pepper, and clam juice. Let stand for 30 minutes before serving.

To roast shallots: Preheat oven to 350° F. Peel the shallots and place in a small baking pan. Roast for 20 to 30 minutes or until golden brown and soft.

Bibb Lettuce Salad with Dijon Mustard & Champagne Vinaigrette

1 small clove garlic
Dash salt and freshly ground black pepper
$1/4$ cup virgin olive oil
3 teaspoons champagne vinegar
1 teaspoon pommery mustard
1 head fresh Bibb lettuce, rinsed and dried

In a large bowl, crush the garlic. Add the salt, black pepper, oil, and vinegar and whisk together until well blended. Add the mustard and whisk again. Let stand for 10 minutes.

Adjust oil/vinegar ratio to taste. Just before serving, add the lettuce and toss together. Serve chilled.

YIELD: 4 SERVINGS

Ratatouille

5 tablespoons olive oil
1 medium onion, thinly sliced
2 cloves garlic, finely chopped
1 pound 12 ounces eggplant, peeled, sliced, and quartered
1 medium zucchini, sliced and quartered
1 medium red bell pepper, seeded, deveined, and chopped
1 1/2 cups chopped fresh Italian plum or Roma tomatoes
1/4 teaspoon dried oregano
1/4 teaspoon dried thyme
1/8 teaspoon ground coriander
1/4 teaspoon fennel seeds
3/4 teaspoon salt
Freshly ground black pepper to taste
1/2 cup chopped fresh basil

In a large skillet, heat 2 tablespoons of the oil and sauté the onion and garlic on medium heat for 3 to 5 minutes, or until the onion is tender.

Add the remaining oil and increase the heat to medium-high. Add the eggplant and cook, stirring occasionally, for 10 to 14 minutes, or until the eggplant is softened.

Stir in the zucchini and bell pepper and cook on medium heat, stirring occasionally, for 12 minutes. Stir in the tomatoes and cook for 5 to 7 minutes or until tender. Stir in the oregano, thyme, coriander, fennel seeds, salt, black pepper, and basil and cook for 1 minute, stirring constantly. Serve immediately.

YIELD: 4 SERVINGS

Bailey's Irish Cream Cheese Torte

Crust:
2 1/2 cups chocolate cookie crumbs
1/2 cup melted unsalted butter or more

Filling:
Three 8-ounce packages cream cheese, at room temperature
1 1/4 cups granulated sugar
4 eggs
1/2 cup sour cream
1/2 cup Bailey's Irish Cream liqueur
1 to 2 cups chopped fresh tart cherries

To make the crust: In a medium-sized bowl, mix together the crumbs with enough melted butter to hold together. Press the crumb mixture into the bottom and up the sides of a 9-inch springform pan. Chill in the freezer until the filling is ready.

Preheat oven to 350° F. To make the filling: In a large bowl, beat the cream cheese with an electric mixer for 2 minutes or until smooth. Slowly beat in the sugar. Add the eggs, one at a time, beating well after each addition. Add the sour cream and liqueur and mix well.

Pour half of the batter into the chilled crust. Gently layer the cherries over the batter. Pour the remaining batter over the top and bake for 1 hour or until set.

Let cool in the pan for 15 to 20 minutes before chilling overnight. Serve chilled.

YIELD: 8 SERVINGS

Butternut Squash Soup

1 large butternut squash
1 tablespoon butter
1 large onion, chopped
3 stalks celery, chopped
4 quarts chicken stock
1 teaspoon freshly ground white pepper
1 teaspoon ground nutmeg
Salt to taste

Preheat oven to 350° F. Cut the squash lengthwise, scrape out the seeds and fibrous center, and reserve the seeds. Place the squash halves in a baking pan skin-side up in 1 inch of water and bake for 45 to 60 minutes or until semisoft. Remove and let cool. Remove the skin and mash the squash meat. Set aside.

In a large, heavy-bottomed pot, melt the butter and sauté the onion and celery for 3 to 6 minutes, or until the onion is translucent. Add the mashed squash meat and the stock and bring to a boil. Reduce heat to simmer and cook for 1 hour.

To roast the reserved squash seeds: Clean the seeds and season with salt. Place the seeds in a small baking pan and bake for 2 to 3 minutes or until golden, stirring once. Remove and let cool.

In a blender or food processor, puree the hot squash mixture in batches, adding the white pepper, nutmeg, and salt. Return the mixture to the pot and reheat.

Ladle the soup into bowls and sprinkle each serving with the roasted seeds. Serve immediately.

YIELD: 6 TO 8 SERVINGS

Pan-Seared Tournedos of Bison with Cabernet Sauvignon Sauce

1 recipe *Cabernet Sauvignon Sauce* (see recipe below)
4 slices wood-smoked bacon
Four 6-ounce bison tenderloin steaks, well trimmed
Olive oil

Wrap the bacon around the outside edge of the steaks, securing the bacon with two ends of a broken toothpick. Lightly brush the steaks with the oil. Place the steaks in a large, hot cast-iron skillet and cook, searing both sides and turning often until medium-rare, about 7 to 10 minutes. Also turn the steaks on the edges to slightly brown the bacon.

Ladle the *Cabernet Sauvignon Sauce* on each plate and place 1 steak on the sauce. Serve immediately.

YIELD: 4 SERVINGS

Cabernet Sauvignon Sauce

6 tablespoons butter
1/2 cup diced carrots
1/2 cup coarsely chopped shallots
1 clove garlic, finely chopped
1/4 cup balsamic vinegar
1/4 cup brandy

1 bottle (750 ml) cabernet sauvignon wine
1 teaspoon dried thyme
1 teaspoon dried sage
1 bay leaf
2 to 3 cups demi-glaze (rich brown sauce)

In a large saucepan, melt 2 tablespoons of the butter and sauté the carrots and shallots for 5 to 7 minutes. Add the garlic and sauté for 3 to 5 minutes. Add the vinegar and reduce until thick. Add the brandy and reduce again.

Stir in the wine and herbs and bring to a boil. Reduce heat to medium and slowly reduce by half. Strain off solids and return the mixture to the saucepan. Return to a boil, gradually adding the demi-glaze to taste. Simmer and thicken with the remaining butter.

Chocolate Mousse Terrine with Raspberry Coulis

1 pound 8 ounces Callebaut dark chocolate (or best quality available)
6 teaspoons warm, strong, brewed coffee
2 cups heavy cream
1 tablespoon confectioners' sugar
6 egg whites
4 egg yolks, well beaten
1 recipe *Raspberry Coulis* (see recipe below)
¹/₂ cup melted *Dark Chocolate Ganache* (see recipe below)
1 recipe *Candela Cream* (see recipe below)
Fresh raspberries, rinsed
Fresh mint leaves, rinsed

In the top of a large double boiler over simmering water, melt the chocolate until soft. Whisk in the coffee, stirring constantly. Remove from heat and whisk until silky smooth. Keep slightly warm.

In a medium-sized bowl, whip together the cream and sugar with an electric mixer until peaks form. In a small bowl, beat the egg whites with an electric mixer until stiff peaks form. Set aside.

Into the chocolate mixture, fold in the egg yolks, then the reserved egg whites, and finally the whipped cream. Spread the mixture into a plastic wrapped-lined 9 x 5-inch loaf pan or flat-bottomed mold. (If have too much mixture for the pan, pour into small ramekins.) Freeze for 1 to 2 hours.

When frozen hard, turn out the terrine onto a work surface and remove the plastic wrap. Coat the sides and top with the *Dark Chocolate Ganache* and return to the freezer. (The ganache coating will set in 10 minutes.)

Remove the terrine from the freezer 5 to 10 minutes before serving. Ladle 2 tablespoons *Raspberry Coulis* on each dessert plate. Slice the terrine with a hot knife. Place 1 slice on the coulis. Garnish each with *Candela Cream*, raspberries, and mint leaves and serve immediately.

YIELD: 8 SERVINGS

Raspberry Coulis

2 pints fresh or frozen (thawed) raspberries
1 teaspoon pure vanilla extract
$^1/_2$ to $^3/_4$ cup granulated sugar or to taste
Cornstarch

In a small saucepan, place the raspberries and cover with warm tap water until all but the top layer of the raspberries are covered and bring to a boil. Reduce heat to simmer and cook, stirring constantly, for 10 to 15 minutes, or until the pulp separates from the seeds and the raspberries are well steeped.

Strain the seeds and pulp from the liquid and return the liquid to the saucepan. Bring to a second boil and add the vanilla and sugar, stirring constantly.

When the sugar has completely dissolved, stir in a small amount of the cornstarch dissolved in water and cook for 5 minutes more or until thickened. Strain and chill before serving.

Dark Chocolate Ganache

8 ounces Callebaut dark chocolate (or best quality available)
$^3/_4$ cup heavy cream
Dash favorite liqueur

In the top of a double boiler over simmering water, slowly melt the chocolate until very soft. Stir in the cream and add the liqueur. Immediately remove from heat and chill. Reheat as needed.

Candela Cream

2 cups chilled heavy cream
$^1/_2$ cup confectioners' sugar
Dash pure vanilla extract

In a medium-sized bowl, whip together all of the ingredients with an electric mixer until stiff peaks form. Use immediately.

Crab Mousse Roulade & Cucumber Slices with Dill Butter

1 pound fresh crabmeat, cartilage removed
2 eggs, slightly beaten
$1/2$ cup pureed summer squash
3 scallions, chopped
$1/2$ cup cracker crumbs
1 tablespoon Old Bay Seasoning
1 to 2 tablespoons fresh lemon juice
7 sheets phyllo pastry, thawed
Shredded fresh Parmesan cheese
Ground pecans
1 recipe *Cucumber Slices with Dill Butter* (see recipe below)

Preheat oven to 350° F. Grease a 9 x 13-inch baking pan. In a medium-sized bowl, combine the first seven ingredients and mix together well. Set aside.

Lightly spray the first sheet of pastry with cooking spray. Sprinkle the sheet lightly with the cheese and cover with a second sheet of pastry. Spray the second sheet and sprinkle lightly with the pecans. Spraying each sheet, alternate the cheese and pecans for the remaining sheets.

Mold the reserved crab mixture in a row on the long edge of the layered pastry facing you and roll all seven sheets to form a tube around the crab mixture. Place in the prepared pan and bake for 15 to 20 minutes or until golden brown.

There were very few dishes prepared on the set of "Inn Country Chefs" more appreciated by the staff than this one. The delicious combination of sautéed cucumber and blue crab is a rare medley perhaps, but one you will repeat often in your own kitchen.

Cut into 1-inch strudels and serve warm with the *Cucumber Slices with Dill Butter*.

YIELD: VARIABLE APPETIZER SERVINGS

Cucumber Slices with Dill Butter

3 large cucumbers, peeled
Salt and freshly ground white pepper to taste
2 to 3 tablespoons butter
2 to 3 tablespoons finely chopped fresh dill

Slice the cucumbers in half lengthwise and scoop out the seeds. Cut the halves into $1/2$-inch slices and lightly season with the salt and white pepper.

In large sauté pan, melt the butter and sauté the cucumber slices on medium-high heat, stirring frequently, for 4 to 5 minutes or until tender-crisp. Toss with the dill and add more butter, if needed. Serve warm. Makes 4 servings.

Fresh Fruit Tart with Mascarpone Cream

1 cup granulated sugar
1 egg
1 teaspoon pure vanilla extract
Dash ground cinnamon
1 cup (2 sticks) unsalted butter, melted
2 cups all-purpose flour
$^1/_2$ cup apricot preserves
3 ripe kiwifruit, peeled and sliced
$^1/_2$ pint fresh raspberries, rinsed
$^1/_2$ pint fresh blackberries, rinsed
$^1/_2$ pint fresh blueberries, rinsed
$^1/_2$ pint fresh strawberries, rinsed, hulled, and sliced

Mascarpone Cream:
1 cup granulated sugar
1 egg
$^1/_2$ teaspoon pure almond extract, or 1 tablespoon Amaretto liqueur
1 pound mascarpone cheese

Preheat oven to 375° F. Butter a shallow 12-inch tart pan and set aside.

In a medium-sized bowl, beat together the sugar and egg until pasty. Whisk in the vanilla, cinnamon, and 2 tablespoons or more of the butter until smooth and slightly liquid. Fold in the flour and add the remaining butter as needed. Knead the dough until all of the ingredients are well combined and the dough forms a firm ball.

Press the dough into the reserved prepared pan and bake for 15 to 20 minutes or until golden brown and firm. (Do not overbake.) Let cool on a wire rack. Spread the preserves evenly over the bottom of the cooled crust and set aside.

To make the mascarpone cream: In another bowl, beat together the sugar, egg, and almond extract with an electric mixer and add the cheese in batches until smooth.

Spread the mixture onto the glazed crust and fill the tart evenly. Cover the filling with a pattern of the fresh fruit and chill for 30 minutes. Serve chilled.

YIELD: 6 TO 8 SERVINGS

Chapter 5

Roasted Lobster with Garlic Crisps & Citrus-Cilantro Viniagrette

Grilled-Roasted Loins of Lamb
with Mint Vinaigrette & Grilled Porcini Mushrooms

Galantine of White Chocolate
with Fresh Berries & Dark Chocolate Sauce

Tomato & Leek Bisque with Romano Gougéres

Seared Yellowfin Tuna
with Thai Pepper Coulis & Roasted Eggplant Relish

Macadamia & Fresh Peach Tarts

Poached Medallions of Black Pearl Salmon
with Tomato & Vidalia Onion Relish

Roasted Tenderloins of Bison & Hot Mushroom Salad

Lemon Pots-de-Crème with Roasted Hazelnut Tuiles

Essence of Asparagus Soup with Crab Corn Cakes

Individual Tarts with White Chocolate Sauce

CHEF CRAIG HARTMAN
Clifton—The Country Inn, Charlottesville, Virginia

MICHAEL CUNNINGHAM

CHEF CRAIG HARTMAN
Clifton—The Country Inn,
Charlottesville, Virginia

Just a few miles from Thomas Jefferson's Monticello, near Charlottesville, Virginia, is a Nationally Registered home that once belonged to one of Jefferson's daughters. Clifton—The Country Inn has long been one of our viewers' favorite inns. Magnificently restored and updated with all of the modern conveniences, Clifton has perhaps the finest country inn kitchen east of the Mississippi River.

Culinary Institute of America alumnus Craig Hartman and his wife Donna are the innkeepers and trustees of the Clifton heritage. Craig wears a second hat, a toque in fact, in his other role as Executive Chef of the inn. Together, the Hartmans take their responsibility of overseeing this Nationally Registered Historic Landmark very seriously, and their award-winning gourmet restaurant follows very much true to form.

As a result of their efforts, Clifton—The Country Inn has received considerable national attention and well-deserved acclaim. In addition to "Inn Country USA" and "Inn Country Chefs" television series, Clifton has been featured in a wide array of print publications, including *Harper's Hideaway Report*, *International Living*, the *Baltimore Sun*, and the *Washington Post*. Inevitably, the media finds their way to Chef Hartman's kitchen and to the elegant food presentations that are uniquely his own.

Roasted Lobster with Garlic Crisps & Citrus-Cilantro Viniagrette

Two 1 ¹/₂-pound cold water lobsters
1 recipe *Garlic Crisps* (see recipe below)
1 recipe *Citrus-Cilantro Vinaigrette* (see recipe below)
2 blood oranges, peeled and sectioned
Fresh cilantro flowers

Start a hickory fire in a home smoker or in a charcoal grill and let burn down to a large bed of red embers. Place the lobsters on the grill, cover, and cook for about 20 minutes. Remove the lobsters and immediately refrigerate.

When the lobsters cool, remove the claws and tail meat, keeping intact. Slice the tails into 6 slices.

Ladle ¹/₄ cup *Citrus-Cilantro Vinaigrette* on each plate. Arrange the lobster (3 slices of tail and 1 claw per serving) on top of the vinaigrette. Place 2 to 3 *Garlic Crisps* like a tepee on the rim of each plate. Arrange the orange sections around the lobster and garnish with the flowers. Serve.

YIELD: 4 APPETIZER SERVINGS

Garlic Crisps

3 tablespoons finely chopped garlic
4 tablespoons olive oil
3 sheets phyllo pastry, thawed
Salt and freshly ground white pepper to taste

Preheat oven to 400° F. In a small bowl, combine the garlic and oil. Brush 1 tablespoon of the garlic mixture on a clean work surface. Lay 1 sheet of the pastry down on top of the oiled surface, brush with the garlic mixture, and season with the salt and white pepper.

Repeat the procedure with the remaining pastry sheets. Cut the layered sheets into uniform triangles. Place on a baking sheet and bake for 7 to 8 minutes or until golden brown.

Citrus-Cilantro Vinaigrette

Juice of 4 blood oranges*
1/4 cup finely chopped shallots
2 tablespoons chopped fresh cilantro
1/2 teaspoon rice vinegar
1/2 fresh Super Chili chili pepper, finely chopped
1/4 teaspoon freshly cracked black peppercorns
Pinch salt

In a small bowl, whisk together all of the ingredients. Adjust the seasonings.

*The juice from 1 orange, 1 lemon, and 1 grapefruit can be substituted for the juice from 4 blood oranges.

Grilled-Roasted Loins of Lamb with Mint Vinaigrette & Grilled Porcini Mushrooms

Two 2- to 3-pound boneless loins of
  lamb (Summerfield Farms, if
  available)
Salt and freshly ground black pepper
Granulated sugar
Olive oil
1 recipe *Mint Vinaigrette* (see recipe
  below)
1 tablespoon white truffle oil*
4 large fresh porcini mushrooms,
  rinsed, trimmed, and cut into $1/8$-
  inch thick slices
$1/2$ clove garlic, finely chopped
1 tablespoon chopped fresh chives
Salt and freshly ground black pepper
  to taste
Granulated sugar to taste
1 tablespoon sherry
Fresh mint leaves, rinsed

One of the wonderful bonuses associated with the rapidly expanding world of country inns and bed & breakfasts in the United States is the general public's discovery of local suppliers, such as Summerfield Farms in Virginia. The media attention that is focused on well-operated inns invariably spills over to the purveyors of everything from fresh meats to produce to folk art. The lamb and veal being produced by Summerfield Farms is a regular staple in Craig's kitchen for a very good reason. It is superb.

Season the lamb with a liberal amount of the salt, black pepper, and sugar and brush with the olive oil. Place the lamb on a broiler pan and grill under the broiler for about 5 minutes on each side. Remove from heat and let stand for 5 to 10 minutes.

In a large sauté pan, heat the truffle oil and sauté the mushrooms, garlic, chives, salt, black pepper, and sugar for 5 to 7 minutes, or until the mushrooms are semicooked. Stir in the sherry and cook for 3 to 5 minutes more.

Ladle $1/4$ cup *Mint Vinaigrette* on each hot plate and slice the loins about $1/8$ inch thick. Shingle half of a loin over the top of the vinaigrette and place some of the mushrooms over the top of the lamb. Garnish with the mint leaves and serve immediately.

Item is available in gourmet foods stores.

YIELD: 4 SERVINGS

Mint Vinaigrette

2 cups loosely packed whole fresh mint leaves
1 clove garlic, finely chopped
2 shallots, peeled
2 teaspoons freshly grated Romano cheese
$^1/_4$ cup balsamic vinegar
2 tablespoons chopped walnuts
Salt and freshly ground black pepper to taste
Granulated sugar to taste
$^1/_4$ cup extra-virgin olive oil

In a blender or food processor, combine all of the ingredients and blend until smooth. Adjust the seasonings.

Galantine of White Chocolate with Fresh Berries & Dark Chocolate Sauce

4 ounces white chocolate
1 envelope unflavored gelatin
3 tablespoons cold water
1 egg
1 egg yolk
$1/4$ cup granulated sugar
1 tablespoon Chambord liqueur
$3/4$ cup whipping cream
1 cup rinsed fresh berries (any type)
1 cup chopped roasted hazelnuts
4 chocolate curls

Dark Chocolate Sauce:
$1/2$ cup whipping cream
4 ounces dark chocolate

To roast hazelnuts: Preheat oven to 350° F. In a small baking pan, place the hazelnuts and bake for 20 minutes or until golden, stirring frequently.

In the top of a double boiler over simmering water, melt the white chocolate. Keep warm. In a small bowl, sprinkle the gelatin over the cold water and let dissolve. In a stainless steel bowl, combine the egg, egg yolk, sugar, and liqueur and whip together over a simmering water bath until the mixture reaches the ribbon stage. Stir the dissolved gelatin into the hot egg mixture and fold in the warm, melted white chocolate until smooth. Let cool.

Whip the $3/4$ cup cream. Fold the whipped cream into the cooled white chocolate mixture. When the mousse has started to set, assemble the galantine.

Lay a sheet of plastic wrap on a work surface. Fold the berries into the mousse. Place the mousse onto the plastic wrap and roll into a cylinder. Fasten the ends and place in the freezer. After the galantine begins to set up, remove from the freezer and place in the refrigerator. Chill for 4 hours.

To make the dark chocolate sauce: In a small saucepan, heat the $1/2$ cup cream to scald and add the dark chocolate, stirring constantly until smooth.

Slice the chilled galantine into 1-inch thick slices. Ladle 2 tablespoons of the chocolate sauce on each dessert plate and place 1 slice of the galantine on top of the sauce. Garnish with the hazelnuts and chocolate curls. Serve immediately.

YIELD: 4 SERVINGS

Tomato & Leek Bisque with Romano Gougères

1 recipe *Romano Gougères* (see recipe below)
2 tablespoons extra-virgin olive oil
2 cups sliced leeks
4 cups diced fresh tomatoes
Salt and freshly cracked black peppercorns to taste
Granulated sugar to taste
$^1\!/_2$ cup white wine
$^1\!/_2$ cup finely chopped fresh basil
$^1\!/_2$ cup vegetable stock

In a medium-sized pot, heat the oil on medium-low heat and sauté the leeks for 3 minutes. (Do not caramelize the leeks.) Add the tomatoes, salt, cracked pepper, and sugar and cook for 8 minutes. Stir in the wine, basil, and stock and simmer until the leeks are soft.

In a blender or food processor, puree the leek mixture until smooth. Adjust the seasonings.

Ladle the bisque into bowls and top with the *Romano Gougères*. Serve immediately.

YIELD: 4 SERVINGS

Romano Gougères

$^1\!/_4$ cup water
2 tablespoons butter
$^1\!/_4$ teaspoon salt
Pinch freshly ground white pepper
Pinch ground nutmeg
$^1\!/_4$ cup all-purpose flour
$^1\!/_4$ cup freshly grated Romano cheese
2 eggs, at room temperature
Egg wash

Preheat oven to 425° F. In a medium-sized saucepan, bring the water, butter, salt, white pepper, and nutmeg to a boil. When the butter has melted, remove from heat. Add the flour and beat with a wooden spoon until the dough pulls away from the sides. Add the cheese and mix together until well combined. Add the eggs, one at a time, and mix together until well combined.

With a tablespoon, scoop out pieces of the dough (the size of an egg) and place the pieces one against the other in a circle in a greased glass pie pan. Brush the egg wash over the dough and bake for 15 to 20 minutes. Let cool on a wire rack.

Seared Yellowfin Tuna with Thai Pepper Coulis & Roasted Eggplant Relish

Four 5-ounce tuna steaks, trimmed
2 tablespoons sesame oil, divided
Salt and freshly ground black pepper
Granulated sugar
1 recipe *Roasted Eggplant Relish* (see recipe below)
1 recipe *Thai Pepper Coulis* (see recipe below)
Fresh chives, chopped

Brush the steaks with 1 tablespoon of the oil and season with the salt, black pepper, and sugar. Refrigerate.

In a large sauté pan, heat the remaining oil to very hot and sear the steaks on both sides, then cook to desired doneness.

Ladle ¼ cup *Thai Pepper Coulis* in the center of each plate and place 1 steak on top of the coulis. Place ¼ cup *Roasted Eggplant Relish* on top of each steak and garnish with the chives. Serve immediately.

YIELD: 4 SERVINGS

Roasted Eggplant Relish

2 tablespoons sesame oil, divided
1 small eggplant
1 teaspoon chopped garlic
2 teaspoons finely chopped fresh gingerroot
2 scallions, sliced
1 teaspoon sliced Thai pepper
2 tablespoons tamari soy sauce
1 tablespoon brown sugar
1 tablespoon fresh lime juice
1 tablespoon chopped fresh cilantro

When you hear the word fusion in conjunction with recipes today, it generally refers to the fusion of cultures and styles of cuisine. Chef Hartman's yellowfin tuna is one of an assortment of terrifically "fused" dishes that he has created in the Clifton kitchen.

Preheat oven to 475° F. Rub 1 tablespoon of the oil on the outside of the eggplant and poke holes through the skin. Place in a baking pan and bake for 25 to 40 minutes. Turn the eggplant over after 15 minutes and continue baking. Remove and let cool.

Peel the skin from the cooled eggplant and puree the pulp in a blender or food processor. Set aside.

In a medium-sized saucepan, heat the remaining oil and sauté the garlic, gingerroot, scallions, and Thai pepper for 3 to 5 minutes. Stir in the remaining ingredients and bring to a boil. Reduce heat to simmer. Add the reserved pureed eggplant and cook for about 5 minutes. Adjust the seasonings.

Thai Pepper Coulis

1 tablespoon sesame oil
2 medium red bell peppers, seeded, deveined, and finely chopped
1 small onion, finely chopped
1 teaspoon finely chopped fresh gingerroot
$^1/_2$ tablespoon finely chopped garlic
2 tablespoons rice vinegar
1 Thai pepper, thinly sliced
Salt and freshly ground black pepper to taste
Granulated sugar to taste

In a small saucepan, heat the oil on medium-low heat, layer the remaining ingredients on the oil, and cover. Cook, stirring frequently, for 4 to 6 minutes, or until the vegetables are tender.

In a blender or food processor, puree the vegetable mixture until smooth. Adjust the seasonings.

Macadamia & Fresh Peach Tarts

4 fresh ripe peaches, peeled and sliced
$1/2$ cup bottled apricot glaze, melted

Macadamia Filling:
$1/4$ cup ($1/2$ stick) butter
$1/2$ cup macadamia nut powder*
$1/4$ cup cream
$1/2$ cup confectioners' sugar
1 egg
2 teaspoons cornstarch
1 teaspoon dark rum
$1/2$ cup whipped cream

Short Dough:
2 cups all-purpose flour
$1/4$ cup ground macadamia nuts
1 tablespoon granulated sugar
1 cup (2 sticks) butter
1 egg
1 tablespoon milk

To make the filling: In a medium-sized bowl, cream the butter. Mix in the nut powder and cream, frequently scraping the sides of the bowl. Add the sugar and egg and beat until fluffy. Add the cornstarch and rum and mix well. Fold in the whipped cream.

Preheat oven to 375° F. To make the dough: Prepare the dough ingredients like pie dough. (Do not overmix.) Roll out the dough to $1/4$ inch thick.

Line individual tart pans with the dough and fill with the macadamia filling. Arrange the sliced peaches on top of the filling in a uniform pattern and bake for about 15 minutes or until set. Remove and brush the glaze over the tarts. Let cool slightly on wire racks. Serve warm.

Item is available in gourmet foods stores.

YIELD: 4 TARTS

Poached Medallions of Black Pearl Salmon with Tomato & Vidalia Onion Relish

1 recipe *Tomato & Vidalia Onion Relish* (see recipe below)
2 cups dry white wine
Salt and freshly cracked black peppercorns
Granulated sugar
1 pound black pearl salmon, cut into 1/2-inch thick medallions
1 envelope unflavored gelatin
3 tablespoons cold water
21-year-old balsamic vinegar*
Fresh parsley, chopped
4 scallion flowers

In a large skillet, bring the wine to a simmer and lightly season with the salt, cracked pepper, and sugar. Place the salmon in the simmering wine, keeping the medallions flat, and poach for about 3 minutes. Remove the medallions from the poaching liquid and place on a baking sheet. Refrigerate. Strain the poaching liquid through a fine-mesh strainer and set aside.

In a small bowl, sprinkle the gelatin over the cold water and let dissolve. When dissolved, add the gelatin to the strained poaching liquid and stir until well blended. Let cool until almost set, then brush the gelatin mixture over the cooled medallions.

Place one-fourth of the *Tomato & Vidalia Onion Relish* slightly off center of each plate and shingle 2 salmon medallions off the relish. Drizzle the 21-year-old vinegar around the medallions and garnish with the parsley and 1 flower. Serve immediately.

Item is available in gourmet foods stores.

YIELD: 4 SERVINGS

Tomato & Vidalia Onion Relish

2 large ripe fresh tomatoes, cut into small uniform dice
1/2 medium Vidalia onion, cut into small uniform dice
1/4 cup chopped fresh parsley
4 tablespoons chopped fresh chives
Salt and freshly cracked black peppercorns to taste
Granulated sugar to taste
1/4 cup balsamic vinegar

In a medium-sized bowl, combine all of the ingredients and mix together well. Adjust the seasonings.

Roasted Tenderloins of Bison & Hot Mushroom Salad

One 5-pound tenderloin of bison, cleaned (Georgetown Farms, if available)
Salt and freshly cracked black peppercorns
Granulated sugar
2 tablepoons extra-virgin olive oil
1 recipe *Hot Mushroom Salad* (see recipe below)

Stuffing:
1 cup coarsely chopped rehydrated sun-dried tomatoes
4 cloves garlic, coarsely chopped
1 medium onion, coarsely chopped
1/4 cup extra-virgin olive oil
2 tablespoons balsamic vinegar
1/4 cup freshly grated Romano cheese
Salt and freshly cracked black peppercorns to taste
Granulated sugar to taste
2 cups finely chopped fresh basil
1 cup small-diced mozzarella cheese

Season the tenderloin with a liberal amount of the salt, cracked pepper, and sugar. In a deep skillet, heat the oil to very hot and sear the tenderloin on all sides.

To make the stuffing: Place the first eight ingredients in a food processor and pulse for 6 pulses. Remove and place the mixture in a large bowl. Stir in the remaining ingredients and mix together well.

Preheat oven to 425° F. To stuff the tenderloin: Cut the seared tenderloin in half across the center. Use a boning knife to make a hole through the center, end to end. With fingers, increase the size of the cavity and fill the cavity with the stuffing. Place in a baking pan and bake for 20 to 25 minutes. Let stand for 5 minutes before slicing.

Divide the tenderloin slices and the *Hot Mushroom Salad* among the plates and serve immediately.

YIELD: 8 TO 10 SERVINGS

Hot Mushroom Salad

$1/2$ cup extra-virgin olive oil
2 large onions, diced
4 cloves garlic, finely chopped
2 quarts sliced fresh mushrooms (shiitake, portobello, oyster, or porcini)
Salt and freshly cracked black peppercorns to taste
Granulated sugar to taste
1 cup balsamic vinegar
$1/4$ cup chopped fresh parsley
$1/4$ cup chopped fresh chives
$1/4$ cup chopped fresh basil
$1/4$ cup chopped fresh thyme

In a large, deep skillet, heat the oil to almost smoking and sauté the onions and garlic for 1 to 2 minutes. Reduce heat slightly. Add the mushrooms, salt, cracked pepper, and sugar and sauté until the mushrooms are tender. Stir in the vinegar and simmer for 3 to 5 minutes. Add all of the herbs and mix together well. Serve hot.

To rehydrate sun-dried tomatoes: Spread the tomatoes on a baking sheet and spray with hot water. Let stand for 15 to 20 minutes; spray again. Repeat this procedure until the tomatoes have plumped to the thickness of fresh tomatoes. This will take about 1 hour.

Lemon Pots-de-Crème with Roasted Hazelnut Tuiles

Juice of 4 lemons
1/2 cup granulated sugar
6 egg yolks, slightly beaten
2 cups half-and-half

1 recipe *Roasted Hazelnut Tuiles* (see recipe below)
Whipped cream
Fresh raspberries, rinsed
Zest of 4 lemons

In a small saucepan, combine the lemon juice and sugar and bring to a boil. Reduce heat to simmer and cook, stirring constantly, until the sugar is dissolved. Let cool.

In a large bowl, combine the cooled sugar mixture and the egg yolks and whisk together well. In a small saucepan, heat the half-and-half to a scald, then slowly add to the egg yolk mixture.

Preheat oven to 250° F. Divide the mixture among 4 ramekins and bake in a water bath for 1 hour or until set. Let cool.

Garnish the pots-de-crème with the whipped cream, raspberries, and lemon zest and place one on each plate. Arrange 3 *Roasted Hazelnut Tuiles* on each plate and serve.
YIELD: 4 SERVINGS

Roasted Hazelnut Tuiles

6 tablespoons (3/4 stick) butter
1/2 cup confectioners' sugar
2 egg whites

1/3 cup all-purpose flour
1/2 cup finely ground roasted hazelnuts (see box on page 69)

In a medium-sized bowl, cream together the butter and sugar. Add the egg whites and mix until well blended. Stir in the flour and hazelnuts and mix together well. Scrape the sides of the bowl and mix for 2 minutes more. Chill for 1 hour.

Preheat oven to 350° F. Place dollops of the chilled batter on a hot greased baking sheet. Thinly spread out each dollop and bake for 7 to 8 minutes or until light golden brown. Gently remove each tuile with a spatula and bend each over a rolling pin to shape. Makes 12 tuiles.

Essence of Asparagus Soup with Crab Corn Cakes

1/2 cup (1 stick) butter

1 large onion, diced

2 bunches fresh asparagus, trimmed and thinly sliced

3 cups chicken or vegetable stock

3 tablespoons cornstarch

2 tablespoons cold water

1 cup cream

Salt and freshly ground white pepper to taste

Granulated sugar to taste

1 recipe *Crab Corn Cakes* (see recipe below)

2 tablespoons chopped fresh parsley

In a large saucepan, melt the butter on medium heat and lightly sauté the onion for 2 to 4 minutes. Add the asparagus and continue to sauté until the asparagus is slightly tender. Add the stock and simmer for about 20 minutes.

In a small bowl, make a slurry with the cornstarch and water. Add the cornstarch mixture to the soup and simmer for at least 5 minutes more. Stir in the cream and add the salt, white pepper, and sugar. Keep warm.

Ladle the soup into bowls and place 2 *Crab Corn Cakes* on top of each serving. Garnish with the parsley and serve immediately.

YIELD: 6 SERVINGS

Crab Corn Cakes

2 ears fresh corn, shucked, cooked, and stripped

1/2 cup cornmeal

1/4 teaspoon baking soda

1/4 teaspoon salt

1 egg, beaten

1/4 cup half-and-half

4 ounces fresh crabmeat, cartilage removed

In a medium-sized bowl, combine the corn, cornmeal, baking soda, and salt. In a small bowl, mix together the egg and half-and-half. Add the egg mixture to the cornmeal mixture and mix until well blended (should resemble pancake batter). Fold in the crabmeat.

Ladle the batter into small circles on a hot griddle and cook until brown on both sides. Makes 12 small corn cakes.

Individual Tarts with White Chocolate Sauce

2 cups all-purpose flour

1 egg, slightly beaten

1 egg white, slightly beaten

$^1/_2$ teaspoon salt

3 tablespoons water

$^2/_3$ cup butter, melted

$^1/_2$ cup granulated sugar

4 medium apples, peeled, quartered, and cut in half

4 tablespoons granulated sugar, divided

8 tablespoons softened butter, divided

1 egg yolk, well beaten

1 recipe *White Chocolate Sauce* (see recipe below)

Fresh raspberries, rinsed

Fresh mint leaves, rinsed

In a large bowl, make a well in the center of the flour. Place the egg, egg white, salt, water, and melted butter in the well. Blend and knead the ingredients into the flour until smooth. Chill the dough for at least 2 hours.

In a small saucepan, caramelize the $^1/_2$ cup sugar. Place one-fourth of the caramelized sugar in each of 4 individual, ceramic tart pans. Immediately pack the apple pieces in the pans uniformly and tightly. Sprinkle 1 tablespoon of the sugar on the top of each pan, then dot each pan with 2 tablespoons of the softened butter.

Preheat oven to 400° F. Roll out the chilled dough and cover each tart with the dough, with an overlap of about $^1/_4$ inch. Crimp the edges and brush the tops with the egg yolk. Cut vents in the tops and bake for 20 to 30 minutes. Remove and let stand for about 10 minutes.

Place 1 tart on each plate and spoon 1 to 2 tablespoons *White Chocolate Sauce* next to the tart. Garnish with the raspberries and mint leaves. Serve immediately.

YIELD: 4 SERVINGS

White Chocolate Sauce

$^1/_4$ cup heavy cream

6 ounces white chocolate

In a small saucepan, heat the cream to a scald and add the dark chocolate, stirring constantly until smooth. Let cool to room temperature.

Chapter 6

Soft-Shell Crab with Spicy Grits

*Grilled Marinated Pork Tenderloin
with Apple, Carrot, & Onion Slaw*

Fresh Berry Strudel

Grilled Barbecued Quail with Creamy Grits

Jumbo Shrimp with Coconut–Curry Sauce

Strawberry-Hazelnut Shortcake

Crayfish Ravioli

Vegetarian Egg Roll Entrée

Lemon Pastel

Hearts of Palm Salad

Striped Bass Stuffed with Seafood Sausage

Southern Pecan Pie with Crème Anglaise & Caramel Sauce

Medallions of Lamb with Dried Cherry-Port Sauce

CHEF KEVIN YOKLEY
The Lords Proprietors' Inn, Edenton, North Carolina

COURTESY THE LORDS PROPRIETORS' INN

CHEF KEVIN YOKLEY
The Lords Proprietors' Inn,
Edenton, North Carolina

Kevin Yokley is a rarity among country inn chefs. A native of the state, where he has studied, apprenticed, and now works, Kevin's grasp of the tastes of the region is superb. His love of hunting and fishing has led him to incorporate fish and game into his creations, which are always complemented by the herbs and seasonal vegetables available in coastal North Carolina. He is responsible for the introduction of dinner service to the lovely Lords Proprietors' Inn in picturesque Edenton, North Carolina.

Innkeepers Arch and Jane Edwards loved the history of their community and their inn, but they realized early in their experience that it was important that they provide enough accommodations to meet the demands of their discriminating guests.

When they needed more guest rooms, they added them. Not by tacking them on to the original historic structure, but by acquiring the houses next door. Eventually, with the addition of a beautifully renovated and spacious old tobacco barn east of the main house, The Lords Proprietors' Inn moved into the full-fledged status of a country inn, with the food and beverage service to go along with the package.

Soft-Shell Crab with Spicy Grits

8 soft-shell crabs, cleaned
Flour
1 tablespoon bacon fat
1 large onion, diced
$^{1}/_{4}$ cup diced celery
1 tablespoon dried oregano
1 tablespoon dried basil
1 teaspoon freshly ground black pepper
$^{1}/_{4}$ teaspoon cayenne pepper
4 cups water
1 cup uncooked grits
Salt to taste
2 tablespoons clarified butter
1 bunch green onions, chopped (white part only)

Dredge the crabs in the flour and set aside.

In a heavy pot, melt the bacon fat and sauté the onion and celery for 3 to 5 minutes, or until the onion is translucent. Stir in the oregano, basil, black pepper, and cayenne pepper. Add the water and bring to a boil. Slowly pour the grits into the water in a steady stream, stirring constantly, and cook for 5 minutes, or until the water is absorbed. Add the salt and keep warm.

In a large, deep skillet, heat the clarified butter and quickly sauté the reserved crabs until golden on both sides.

Place a small mound of grits in the center of each small plate and place 1 crab on top of the grits. Garnish the plate with the green onions and serve immediately.

YIELD: 8 APPETIZER SERVINGS

To make clarified butter: In a small saucepan, melt butter on low heat. Remove from heat and let stand until the solids settle to the bottom. Pour off the top clarified butter into a container and discard the solids.

Grilled Marinated Pork Tenderloin with Apple, Carrot & Onion Slaw

Four 12- to 14-ounce pork
tenderloins

Marinade:
4 cloves garlic
1 tablespoon finely chopped fresh
gingerroot
1 leek (top part only)
3/4 cup fresh lime juice
1/2 cup soy sauce
2 cups corn oil

Pork Stock:
3 tablespoons vegetable oil
2 pounds pork bones
1 pound salt pork ham hock
1 tablespoon bacon fat
1 medium onion, chopped
1 stalk celery, chopped
1 medium carrot, chopped

Slaw:
1/4 cup (1/2 stick) butter
4 medium apples, unpeeled and
julienned
4 medium carrots, julienned
2 medium red onions, julienned
Salt and freshly ground black pepper
to taste

To make the marinade: In a food processor, combine the garlic, ginger, and leek and process until finely chopped. Add the lime juice and soy sauce and blend together. While the processor is running, slowly add the oil.

Place the tenderloins in a shallow, glass baking dish and pour the marinade over the tenderloins. Marinate for 8 hours in the refrigerator.

To make the stock: In a large pot, heat the oil and sauté the bones and ham hock for 10 to 15 minutes or until browned. In a small skillet, heat the bacon fat and brown the onion, celery, and carrot. Add the onion mixture to the browned bones. Add water to cover and simmer for 4 hours.

To make the slaw: In a medium-sized saucepan, melt the butter and sauté the apples, carrots, and onions for 5 to 8 minutes, or until all of the vegetables are tender. Stir in the salt and black pepper. Keep warm.

Over a charcoal fire, grill the marinated tenderloins for 7 minutes on each side. Cut the tenderloins into 1/4-inch slices. Place the warm slaw in a circle on each plate. Place slices of the pork on top of the slaw and drizzle with the pork stock. Serve immediately.

YIELD: 4 SERVINGS

Fresh Berry Strudel

Dough:
3 cups all-purpose flour
3 tablespoons granulated sugar
$1/2$ teaspoon salt
$1/4$ cup vegetable shortening
1 cup (2 sticks) softened butter
$1/4$ cup sour cream
$1/3$ cup water

Filling:
1 pint fresh raspberries, rinsed
1 pint fresh blackberries, rinsed
1 pint fresh blueberries, rinsed
2 tablespoons ground cinnamon
$1/2$ to 1 cup granulated sugar to taste
2 tablespoons cornstarch

Cover a large baking sheet with parchment paper. To make the dough: In a large bowl, mix together the flour, sugar, and salt, then cut in the shortening and butter. Mix in the sour cream and water. Separate the dough in half and roll out each half into a 14 x 16-inch rectangle, $1/8$ inch thick. Set aside.

To make the filling: In a large bowl, gently mix together all of the ingredients. Divide the filling in half.

Preheat oven to 350° F. Spread the short edge of 1 rectangle of the reserved dough with half of the filling. Wrap the dough around the filling. Repeat the procedure with the remaining dough and filling. Place the strudels seam-side down on the prepared baking sheet and bake for 25 minutes or until golden brown. Let cool slightly and cut one strudel into 2-inch slices. Serve warm. Makes 2 strudels.

YIELD: 6 TO 8 SERVINGS

Grilled Barbecued Quail with Creamy Grits

4 semiboneless quail
Salt and freshly ground black pepper
1 recipe *Creamy Grits* (see recipe
 below)
Green onions, chopped (tops only)

Barbecue Sauce:
$^1/_4$ cup white wine
1 tablespoon butter
2 tablespoons brown sugar
1 teaspoon ground mustard
1 bay leaf
3 tablespoons Worcestershire sauce
$^1/_2$ cup tomato paste
1 cup catsup
$^3/_4$ cup finely chopped onions
1 tablespoon fresh lemon juice
$^1/_2$ teaspoon freshly ground black
 pepper
1 teaspoon salt
$^1/_2$ teaspoon cayenne pepper
2 teaspoons chili powder

To make the sauce: In a large pot, mix together all of the ingredients and reduce by one-eighth. Chill for 30 minutes. Marinate the quail in the sauce for 24 hours in the refrigerator. Reserve 1 cup of the sauce.

Split each quail in half, separating down the neck bone vertically. Season with the salt and black pepper. Grill the quail for 2 minutes on each side.

Place 1 scoop of *Creamy Grits* on each plate and top with 1 quail. Drizzle the reserved barbecue sauce on each quail and garnish with the green onion tops. Serve immediately.

YIELD: 8 APPETIZER SERVINGS

Creamy Grits

4 cups chicken stock
1 cup uncooked grits
Salt and freshly ground white pepper
 to taste
1 cup heavy cream

In a large saucepan, bring the stock to a boil. Slowly add the grits and cook, stirring constantly, for 5 minutes or until the stock is absorbed. Reduce heat to simmer. Stir in the salt, white pepper, and cream. Keep warm.

Jumbo Shrimp with Coconut-Curry Sauce

28 jumbo shrimp (10 to 15 count),
  peeled and deveined with tails
Salt
Dash cayenne pepper
2 tablespoons clarified butter (see
  box on page 83)
1 recipe *Coconut-Curry Sauce* (see
  recipe below)

Rice:
2 cups water
1 cup uncooked basmati rice
1 cup heavy cream
Freshly ground white pepper to taste

To make the rice: In a medium-sized saucepan, bring the water to a boil. Add the rice and cook, uncovered, stirring occasionally.

In a small saucepan, heat the cream. Add the hot cream to the rice when the water has been absorbed and season with the salt and white pepper. Cover and let stand for 10 minutes.

Slightly score the shrimp down the back. Lightly season with the salt and cayenne pepper. In a large sauté pan, melt ¹/₂ tablespoon of the butter and sauté 7 of the shrimp for 1 to 2 minutes. Remove and keep warm. Repeat the procedure for the remaining butter and shrimp.

Place a mound of the rice on each plate. Ladle 2 tablespoons *Coconut-Curry Sauce* on the rice and arch 7 shrimp over the top of the rice. Serve immediately.

YIELD: 4 SERVINGS

Coconut-Curry Sauce

1 tablespoon butter
1 tablespoon finely chopped garlic
4 shallots, finely chopped
1 tablespoon finely chopped fresh
  gingerroot
1 teaspoon chili powder
2 teaspoons ground coriander
1 teaspoon ground turmeric
1 cup coconut milk
1 cup heavy cream

In a sauté pan, melt the butter and gently sauté the garlic, shallots, and ginger for 3 to 5 minutes. Stir in the chili powder, coriander, and turmeric. Mix in the milk and cream and reduce the mixture to sauce consistency. Keep warm.

Strawberry-Hazelnut Shortcake

1 quart fresh strawberries, rinsed, hulled, and sliced
Granulated sugar to taste
Whipped cream
Fresh mint leaves, rinsed

Shortcake:
2 cups all-purpose flour
1 tablespoon baking powder
1 tablespoon granulated sugar
1 teaspoon salt
3/4 cup ground hazelnuts
5 tablespoons butter
1 cup heavy cream

To make the shortcake: Cover a baking sheet with parchment paper. In a medium-sized bowl, mix together the first five ingredients until a coarse meal forms. Gently add the butter and cream until the dough just comes together.

Preheat oven to 350° F. Form the dough into two logs. Place the logs on the prepared baking sheet and bake for 25 minutes or until golden brown. Let cool on a wire rack.

In a medium-sized bowl, gently mix together the strawberries and sugar. Cut the cooled shortcake into triangle wedges.

Place a scoop of the sweetened strawberries on each plate and place the small end of the shortcake triangle on top of the strawberries. Place a small scoop of the whipped cream next to the berries and garnish with the mint leaves. Serve immediately.

YIELD: 8 SERVINGS

Crayfish Ravioli

Pasta:
2 ½ cups all-purpose flour
½ teaspoon salt
1 teaspoon dried oregano
1 teaspoon freshly ground black pepper
1 tablespoon olive oil
2 tablespoons tomato paste
3 eggs, beaten

Filling:
1 tablespoon olive oil
1 medium onion, finely chopped
4 fennel bulbs, finely chopped
Freshly ground black pepper to taste
One 12-ounce package crayfish tails,
    thawed*
2 ounces goat cheese
Salt and freshly ground black pepper
    to taste

Sauce:
2 cups heavy cream
1 tablespoon soy sauce
¼ teaspoon ground cloves
¼ cup freshly grated Parmesan cheese

Crayfish (or crawfish as the Cajuns spell it), found primarily in fresh water bayous throughout the southern United States, is a delicacy that looks like a miniature lobster, but possesses a delicious rich flavor somewhere between shrimp, lobster, and heaven. The expanding popularity of crayfish has now led to commercial farming and processing, which ensures its availability year-round. Crayfish tails are readily available in frozen form and work well in Kevin's ravioli recipe.

To make the pasta: In a food processor, combine the first four ingredients until well mixed. Add the oil, tomato paste, and eggs, one at a time, and mix together well. Let the dough rest for 1 hour.

Roll out the dough and use a large ravioli cutter to make squares.

To make the filling: In a large skillet, heat the oil and sauté the onion, fennel, and black pepper for 5 to 6 minutes, or until the onion is browned. Chill.

In a food processor, combine the chilled onion mixture, crayfish tails, and cheese and process until just mixed. Season with the salt and black pepper. Fill the ravioli squares.

To make the sauce: In a small saucepan, combine the cream and soy sauce on medium heat and reduce to a thick sauce. Stir in the cloves and cheese and blend together well. Keep warm.

In a large pot of nearly boiling water with 1 tablespoon olive oil added, simmer the ravioli, 2 to 3 at a time, for 2 minutes. Remove the cooked ravioli and keep warm. Repeat the procedure with the remaining uncooked ravioli.

Ladle 3 tablespoons of the sauce on each small plate and place 1 ravioli on the sauce. Serve immediately.

Item is available in large supermarkets and gourmet foods stores.

YIELD: 8 APPETIZER SERVINGS

Vegetarian Egg Roll Entrée

1 ½ tablespoons butter
8 ounces fresh portobello
   mushrooms, sliced
1 pound bok choy, chopped
1 tablespoon finely chopped garlic
4 ounces goat cheese

2 tablespoons soy sauce
Vegetable oil
One 1-pound package egg roll wrappers
2 to 3 tablespoons vegetable oil
6 medium potatoes, peeled and julienned

In a large skillet, melt the butter and sauté the mushrooms, bok choy, and garlic for 3 to 5 minutes, or until the vegetables are wilted. Add the cheese and soy sauce and stir until the cheese has melted. Chill for 30 minutes.

In a large, deep skillet, heat 2 inches of the oil on medium-high heat. Fill the wrappers with ¼ cup of the chilled mixture and deep-fry until golden brown. Drain on paper towels. Keep warm.

In another skillet, heat the 2 to 3 tablespoons oil and fry the potatoes until crisp. Drain on paper towels and separate into 6 servings.

Place 1 "nest" of potatoes on each plate and place 2 egg rolls on the potatoes. Serve immediately.

YIELD: 6 SERVINGS

Lemon Pastel

1 cup granulated sugar
$^1/_2$ cup fresh lemon juice
3 eggs, slightly beaten
3 egg yolks, slightly beaten
$^1/_2$ cup heavy cream
Fresh mint leaves, rinsed

Fruit Puree:
1 pint fresh raspberries, rinsed
6 tablespoons granulated sugar
2 passion fruit, peeled and coarsely chopped

Whipped Cream:
$^1/_2$ cup heavy cream, whipped
2 tablespoons granulated sugar
Dash pure vanilla extract

Preheat oven to 325° F. In a medium-sized bowl, whisk together the sugar, lemon juice, eggs, and egg yolks. Add the cream and whisk to blend well.

Divide the cream mixture among 4 ramekins. Place the ramekins in a water bath and bake for 1 hour. Chill until ready to serve.

To make the fruit puree: In a blender or food processor, blend together the raspberries and 3 tablespoons of the sugar until smooth. Strain to remove seeds. In a blender or food processor, blend together the passion fruit and remaining sugar. Strain to remove seeds. In a medium-sized bowl, mix together both purees and set aside.

To make the whipped cream: In a medium-sized bowl, gently combine the whipped cream, sugar, and vanilla. Chill.

Ladle 2 tablespoons of the reserved fruit puree in the center of each plate. Carefully remove each pastel from the ramekin and place upside down on top of the puree. Garnish with the whipped cream and top with the mint leaves. Serve immediately.
YIELD: 4 SERVINGS

Hearts of Palm Salad

Two 12-ounce cans hearts of palm, drained and cut into lengthwise strips
1 pound fresh arugula, rinsed and dried
2 medium red bell peppers, seeded, deveined, and diced
2 green onions, sliced
2 medium carrots, diced

Dressing:
2 egg yolks
2 tablespoons catsup
1 shallot, coarsely chopped
1 tablespoon fresh lemon juice
1 cup cottonseed oil
2 tablespoons sesame oil
4 tablespoons olive oil
Salt and freshly ground black pepper to taste

Divide and layer the first five ingredients on 6 salad plates.

To make the dressing: While a food processor is running, add the egg yolks, catsup, shallot, and lemon juice, one at a time, until well combined. Slowly add the oils in order, then add the salt and black pepper.

Drizzle the dressing over the prepared salads and serve immediately.

YIELD: 6 SERVINGS

Striped Bass Stuffed with Seafood Sausage

12 fresh basil leaves, rinsed
4 shallots, peeled
6 ounces fresh bay scallops
6 ounces fresh tuna
1 teaspoon salt
1 teaspoon freshly ground white pepper
Four 6-ounce striped bass fillets, feather bones removed
4 strips bacon
White wine
2 tablespoons butter

Preheat oven to 350° F. In a food processor, coarsely chop the basil and shallots. Add the scallops, tuna, salt, and white pepper and process until ball of seafood forms.

Place the fillets on a work surface and roll each into a circle. Surround each fillet with 1 strip of the bacon, forming a hollow round of bass. Stuff each cavity with the seafood mixture. Place the stuffed fillets in a baking pan and cover with the wine and dot with the butter. Bake, covered, for 25 minutes. Serve immediately.

YIELD: 4 SERVINGS

Creating a rich spicy sausage using seafood is a comparatively recent innovation among country inn chefs. Using that same seafood sausage recipe as a stuffing is an even more recent development. The sausage in this recipe is a fine accent to the firm-fleshed striped bass.

Southern Pecan Pie with Crème Anglaise & Caramel Sauce

1 recipe *Crème Anglaise* (see recipe below)
1 recipe *Caramel Sauce* (see recipe below)
Fresh mint leaves, rinsed

Dough:
2 ¹/₄ cups all-purpose flour
2 tablespoons granulated sugar
1 teaspoon salt
11 tablespoons cold butter
7 tablespoons vegetable shortening
2 tablespoons water

Filling:
4 eggs, beaten
1 cup packed brown sugar
³/₄ teaspoon salt
1 cup (2 sticks) butter, melted
1 cup corn syrup
1 cup pecan pieces
1 ¹/₂ teaspoons pure vanilla extract

To make the dough: In a food processor, combine the flour, sugar, and salt. Add the butter and cut in with five 1-second pulses. Add the shortening and cut in with five 1-second pulses. Add the water and process until the dough forms a ball. Thinly roll out the dough and place in a 9-inch pie pan. Chill.

Preheat oven to 450° F. To make the filling: In a medium-sized bowl, mix together all of the ingredients.

Pour the filling into the chilled pie shell and bake for 12 minutes. Reduce temperature to 350° and bake for 50 minutes more. Let cool on a wire rack.

Place 1 piece of the pie off center on each plate. Ladle ¹/₄ cup *Crème Anglaise* on the side of the pie. Dot the crème with the *Caramel Sauce* and swirl. Garnish with the mint leaves and serve immediately.

YIELD: 6 SERVINGS

Crème Anglaise

2 cups milk
6 egg yolks
¹/₂ cup granulated sugar
1 ¹/₂ teaspoons pure vanilla extract

In the top of a double boiler over simmering water, scald the milk. In a medium-sized bowl, while beating together the egg yolks and sugar with an electric mixer, slowly add the scalded milk and continue beating until thick and light.

Return the mixture to the double boiler and heat slowly, stirring constantly, until the mixture coats the back of a spoon. Remove and place in an ice bath, stirring occasionally. Add the vanilla.

Caramel Sauce

2 cups granulated sugar
¹/₂ cup water
2 cups heavy cream

In a small saucepan, combine the sugar and water and heat until the mixture is caramel colored, stirring frequently. Remove from heat and vigorously whisk in the cream until well blended. Let cool to room temperature.

Medallions of Lamb with Dried Cherry-Port Sauce

Four 7-ounce lamb tenderloins

Marinade:
¹/₂ cup sherry
6 cloves garlic, coarsely chopped
4 shallots, chopped
¹/₄ cup chopped fresh thyme
¹/₂ teaspoon freshly crushed black peppercorns
1 ¹/₂ cups olive oil
1 recipe *Dried Cherry-Port Sauce* (see recipe below)

To make the marinade: In a medium-sized bowl, combine all of the ingredients and mix together well. Rub the tenderloins with the marinade and place in a shallow glass baking dish. Cover and marinate for at least 1 hour or overnight in the refrigerator.

Grill the tenderloins for 8 to 10 minutes for medium rare. Slice into medallions. Ladle ¹/₄ cup *Dried Cherry-Port Sauce* onto each plate and place the medallions over the sauce. Serve immediately.

YIELD: 4 SERVINGS

Dried Cherry-Port Sauce

¹/₂ cup dried cherries
3 cups port wine
¹/₄ cup granulated sugar
2 cups demi-glaze (rich brown sauce)
2 tablespoons cold butter

In a large saucepan, combine the cherries, wine, and sugar and reduce by three-fourths on medium heat. Stir in the demi-glaze and simmer until thick. Mix in the butter until well blended.

Creole Shrimp Cocktail. Chef Sherry Rosemann, Rose Inn.

Pears Poached in Port Wine with Crème Anglaise & Red Wine–Caramel Sauce.
Chef Sherry Rosemann, Rose Inn.

Recipes from Chef Jacques Thiebeult, The Homestead Inn. Clockwise from top: Napoleons of Sea Scallops with Smoked Salmon & Chive Sauce; Soft-Shell Crabs with Lemon, Garlic & Basil.

Roast Loins of Lamb in Black Olive Crust with Port Wine Sauce.
Chef Jacques Thiebeult, The Homestead Inn.

Recipes from Chef Jacques Thiebeult,
The Homestead Inn. Clockwise from
top: Cassoulette d'Escargots; Salmon &
Oyster Tartare.

Heirloom "One-Bite" Butter Biscuits. Chef Deedy Marble, The Governor's Inn.

Recipes from Chef Deedy Marble, The Governor's Inn. Clockwise from top: Wine Broth; National Soup of the Islands of Madeira; Iced Granny Apple.

CRAIG HAMMELL

Pan-Seared Tournedos of Bison with Cabernet Sauvignon Sauce.
Chef Michael Sheehan, Prospect Hill Plantation Inn.

Chocolate Mousse Terrine with Raspberry Coulis.
Chef Michael Sheehan, Prospect Hill Plantation Inn.

Grilled-Roasted Loins of Lamb with Mint Vinaigrette & Porcini Mushrooms.
Chef Craig Hartman, Clifton—The Country Inn.

Poached Medallions of Black Pearl Salmon with Tomato & Vidalia Onion Relish.
Chef Craig Hartman, Clifton—The Country Inn.

Individual Tarts with White Chocolate Sauce.
Chef Craig Hartman, Clifton—The Country Inn.

Medallions of Lamb with Dried Cherry–Port Sauce.
Chef Kevin Yokley, The Lords Proprietors' Inn.

Grilled Scallops with Sunflower Seed–Basil Topping.
Chef Lucy Hamilton, Richmond Hill Inn.

Grilled Salmon with Dilled Berry Relish & Chardonnay Butter Sauce.
Chef Lucy Hamilton, Richmond Hill Inn.

Rice Paper-Wrapped Yellowfin Tuna with Ginger Sauce.
Chef Cory Mattson, The Fearrington House.

MICHAEL CUNNINGHAM

Goat Cheese Salad with Basil Vinaigrette & Mango Salsa. Chef Cory Mattson, The Fearrington House.

MICHAEL CUNNINGHAM

Mixed Grill with Red Wine Vinaigrette. Chef Cory Mattson, The Fearrington House.

Cornmeal–Breaded Trout with Hominy
Hash & Baked Eggs.
Chef John Fleer, Inn at Blackberry Farm.

Moon Pie.
Chef John Fleer, Inn at Blackberry Farm.

FAITH ECHTERMEYER

Pacific Salmon with Rosemary–Mustard Sauce.
Chef Jean–Louis Hamiche, Carter House/Hotel Carter.

Gathering fresh produce from the garden, Carter House/Hotel Carter.

Chapter 7

Crudités Salad

*Grilled Salmon with
Chardonnay Butter Sauce & Dilled Berry Relish*

Lemon-Lime Tart with Coconut Crust

Sauté of Wild Mushrooms & Marsala with Herb-Walnut Toast

*Lamb Chops in Pistachio-Goat Cheese Crust
with Dried Cherry Sauce*

Raspberry Crème Brûlée

Mountain Apple & Vidalia Onion Soup with Garlic Croutons

White Chocolate & Cranberry Brownies

Chicken, Wild Rice & Peach Salad with Lime-Tarragon Dressing

Grilled Scallops with Sunflower Seed-Basil Topping

Lemon Risotto

Sautéed Spinach with Mustard Seeds

"Watermelon" Bombe

CHEF LUCY HAMILTON
Richmond Hill Inn, Asheville, North Carolina

MICHAEL CUNNINGHAM

CHEF LUCY HAMILTON
Richmond Hill Inn,
Asheville, North Carolina

Increasingly country inn chefs are bringing impressive culinary credentials to the table when they join an inn. Lucy Hamilton's contributions to the Richmond Hill Inn graphically reflect her London Cordon Bleu training. Richmond Hill is an elegant four-star crown in the Blue Ridge Mountains near Asheville, North Carolina. Nestled in the trees above the French Broad River, this lovingly restored century-old Queen Anne-style home was originally the home of one of North Carolina's most prominent citizens, Richmond Pearson, a former member of Congress, ambassador, and community leader widely applauded for his political and diplomatic service.

From the massive and rich oak entry foyer, paneled entirely of native oaks from nearby forests, you enter Gabrielle's, Richmond Hill's popular dining room, named after Richmond Pearson's bride. It's here that Lucy Hamilton's innovative touches abound. Chef Hamilton's own interests in training others is one of the reasons that her recipes are so concise, straight forward, and superb!

Crudités Salad

2 medium carrots, peeled
1 medium turnip, peeled
1 celery root, peeled
8 ounces Gruyère cheese
4 tablespoons champagne vinegar
$^{3}/_{4}$ cup olive oil
3 tablespoons Dijon mustard
$^{3}/_{4}$ teaspoon salt
Freshly ground black pepper to taste
Fresh lettuce, rinsed and dried

Using a mandoline or a very sharp knife, slice each vegetable and the cheese into julienne strips. Set aside.

In a large bowl, whisk together the vinegar, oil, mustard, salt, and black pepper. Toss the reserved vegetables and cheese with the dressing and chill for at least 1 hour.

Divide the lettuce among the salad plates and place equal amounts of the vegetable mixture on top of the lettuce. Serve.

YIELD: 6 SERVINGS

Grilled Salmon with Chardonnay Butter Sauce & Dilled Berry Relish

1 recipe *Chardonnay Butter Sauce* (see recipe below)

1 recipe *Dilled Berry Relish* (see recipe below)

12 new potatoes, unpeeled

3 tablespoons butter

Salt and freshly ground black pepper to taste

20 spears fresh asparagus

Four 6-ounce salmon fillets, skin removed

Salt and freshly ground black pepper to taste

Pare the potatoes to look like mushrooms: To make the "stem," insert a corer into each potato two-thirds from the bottom. Leave the corer in place. To make the "mushroom cap," take a paring knife and make a horizontal cut all around the potato to meet the corer. Carefully remove the bottom of the potato, then remove the corer, exposing the "stem."

In a large skillet, melt the butter and sauté/roast the potatoes, salt, and black pepper until the potatoes are lightly browned and tender. Steam the asparagus for 5 to 7 minutes or until tender-crisp. Keep warm.

Season the fillets with the salt and black pepper and grill over hot coals for about 5 minutes on each side or until cooked through.

Ladle 2 to 3 tablespoons *Chardonnay Butter Sauce* onto each plate and place 1 fillet on top of the sauce. At one end of each fillet, place the *Dilled Berry Relish* and the "mushroom" potatoes. Fan 5 asparagus spears by the potatoes and serve immediately.

YIELD: 4 SERVINGS

Chardonnay Butter Sauce

$1/2$ cup chardonnay wine

1 shallot, finely chopped

1 bay leaf

1 tablespoon white wine vinegar

1 teaspoon finely chopped fresh chives

2 tablespoons cream

$1/2$ cup (1 stick) butter, at room temperature

Salt and freshly ground black pepper to taste

In a small saucepan, combine the wine, shallot, bay leaf, vinegar, and chives and cook on low heat until the wine has almost evaporated. Stir in the cream and cook on medium heat, whisking occasionally, until the cream is reduced by half. Strain to remove the shallot, bay leaf, and chives.

On low heat, gradually whisk in the butter until the sauce has thickened. (Do not allow to boil.) Add the salt and black pepper. Keep warm.

Dilled Berry Relish

$1/4$ cup olive oil
2 tablespoons champagne vinegar
2 tablespoons chopped fresh dill
3 kiwifruits, peeled and cut into medium dice
$1/2$ cup fresh blueberries
1 cup sliced fresh strawberries
1 cup fresh raspberries

In a small bowl, whisk together the oil, vinegar, and dill. In a medium-sized bowl, gently combine the kiwifruit, blueberries, strawberries, and raspberries. Pour the dressing over the fruit and toss gently. Chill.

Lemon-Lime Tart with Coconut Crust

Crust:
1 ¹/₂ cups all-purpose flour
¹/₄ cup confectioners' sugar
Pinch salt
6 tablespoons (³/₄ stick) butter,
   divided
2 tablespoons vegetable shortening
¹/₂ cup shredded dried coconut
¹/₂ cup ground almonds
3 tablespoons water

Filling:
1 teaspoon unflavored gelatin
2 tablespoons boiling water
Grated zest of 1 lemon
Grated zest of 2 limes
¹/₄ cup fresh lemon juice
¹/₄ cup fresh lime juice
¹/₄ cup (¹/₂ stick) unsalted butter,
   melted and cooled
1 cup granulated sugar
6 egg yolks

To make the crust: In a food processor, combine the flour, sugar, and salt and pulse to mix together. Add the butter and shortening and continue to pulse until the mixture looks coarse, like oatmeal. Add the coconut, almonds, and water and process briefly, just until the mixture forms a loose ball.

Gather the dough and roll out two-thirds of the dough on a floured surface. Place the dough in a 9-inch, removable bottom tart pan and prick the bottom with a fork. Chill for at least 30 minutes.

Roll out the remaining dough and cut out shapes with a cookie cutter. Place the cutouts on a baking sheet and chill.

To make the filling: In a small bowl, dissolve the gelatin in the boiling water. Set aside.

In a medium-sized nonreactive saucepan, whisk together both zests, both juices, the butter, sugar, and egg yolks and cook on low heat, stirring constantly, until thickened. Remove from heat and stir in the reserved gelatin. Let cool.

Preheat oven to 375° F. Weight down the chilled crust with pie weights or dried beans and bake for 12 minutes. Remove the weights and bake for 10 minutes more or until golden brown. Bake the chilled cutouts for 15 minutes or until golden brown. Let the crust and cutouts cool.

Fill the crust with the filling and garnish with the cutouts. Chill for several hours. Serve.

YIELD: 6 TO 8 SERVINGS

Sauté of Wild Mushrooms & Marsala with Herb-Walnut Toast

8 slices *Herb-Walnut Bread* (see recipe below)
$^1/_4$ cup ($^1/_2$ stick) butter
1 $^1/_2$ cups sliced fresh shiitake mushrooms
$^2/_3$ cup sliced fresh chanterelle mushrooms
$^2/_3$ cup sliced fresh lobster mushrooms
1 teaspoon dried rosemary
Salt and freshly ground black pepper to taste
$^1/_2$ cup Marsala wine
$^1/_2$ cup heavy cream
4 tablespoons freshly grated Parmesan cheese

In a large sauté pan, melt the butter and sauté all of the mushrooms, the rosemary, salt, and black pepper on medium-high heat for 2 minutes. Remove from heat and pour the wine over the mushrooms to deglaze the pan. (Be very careful—the hot pan might cause the wine to ignite.) Return to medium-high heat and cook until the liquid has reduced to about half. Stir in the cream and cook for 2 minutes more, stirring constantly.

Cut each slice of the *Herb-Walnut Bread* diagonally into 2 triangles and place the triangles on a baking sheet. Toast under the broiler until lightly browned on each side.

Arrange 2 toasted triangles on each ovenproof plate and top with the mushroom mixture. Sprinkle with the cheese and place the plates under the broiler to brown the cheese. Serve immediately.

YIELD: 8 APPETIZER SERVINGS

Herb-Walnut Bread

2 tablespoons active dry yeast
2 cups warm water
1 teaspoon granulated sugar
6 cups all-purpose flour
$^2/_3$ cup whole wheat flour
1 tablespoon salt

$^2/_3$ cup olive oil
1 tablespoon dried rosemary
1 tablespoon chopped walnuts
1 tablespoon chopped black truffle
  (optional)
Cornmeal

In a small bowl, sprinkle the yeast over the water. Whisk in the sugar and let stand until bubbly.

In a large bowl, combine 3 cups of the all-purpose flour, all of the whole wheat flour, and the salt. Add the oil and mix together well. Add the yeast mixture, rosemary, walnuts, and truffle. Stir in the remaining all-purpose flour to make a soft dough. Knead until smooth and very elastic. Place the dough in a large, buttered bowl and cover with plastic wrap. Let rise until doubled in bulk, about 2 hours.

Dust 2 baking sheets with the cornmeal. Punch down the dough and divide into 4 pieces. Shape each piece into an 8 x 3-inch loaf and place the loaves on the prepared baking sheets. Cover loosely with a towel and let rise until doubled, about 1 hour.

Preheat oven to 375° F. Bake the bread for 30 minutes or until golden brown. Let cool on a wire rack.

Lamb Chops in Pistachio-Goat Cheese Crust with Dried Cherry Sauce

8 lamb chops, cut 2 inches thick
Salt and freshly ground black pepper to taste
1 cup softened goat cheese
$^1/_2$ cup crushed pistachio nuts
1 recipe *Dried Cherry Sauce* (see recipe below)

Preheat oven to 425° F. Season the chops with the salt and black pepper and coat each side of the chops with the cheese. Press the nuts into the cheese. Place the chops in a roasting pan and roast for 20 minutes or to desired doneness.

Ladle $^1/_4$ cup *Dried Cherry Sauce* into the center of each plate and place 2 lamb chops, with ribs crisscrossed, at the bottom of the plate. Serve immediately.

YIELD: 4 SERVINGS

Dried Cherry Sauce

6 tablespoons granulated sugar
4 tablespoons water
2 tablespoons red wine vinegar
1 cup *Red Wine Sauce* (see recipe below)
$^1/_2$ cup dried cherries
1 $^1/_2$ teaspoons chopped fresh rosemary

In a medium-sized saucepan, combine the sugar and water on low heat and cook, stirring constantly, until the sugar dissolves. Bring the dissolved sugar mixture to a boil and cook until the mixture is a light caramel color. Immediately remove from heat. Let cool slightly.

Stir in the vinegar, *Red Wine Sauce,* and cherries and heat just to the boiling point. Mix in the rosemary. Reduce heat and keep warm.

Red Wine Sauce

3 tablespoons unsalted butter
1 medium carrot, diced
1 stalk celery, diced
1 small onion, diced
1 shallot, finely chopped
1 cup dry red wine
6 cups beef stock
1 medium fresh tomato, chopped
1 bay leaf
$^1/_2$ teaspoon dried thyme
2 whole cloves
10 black peppercorns
2 tablespoons cornstarch dissolved in $^1/_4$ cup cold beef stock
Salt and freshly ground black pepper to taste

In a large saucepan, melt the butter and sauté the carrot, celery, onion, and shallot for 5 to 8 minutes or until tender. Stir in the wine and cook until the liquid has reduced to a glaze. Add the stock, tomato, bay leaf, thyme, cloves, and peppercorns and bring to a boil. Reduce heat to simmer and cook, uncovered, for 2 hours. Strain.

Return the sauce to the saucepan. Stir in the cornstarch mixture and bring to a boil. Add the salt and black pepper. Reduce heat and keep warm, stirring frequently.

Raspberry Crème Brûlée

1 cup fresh or frozen (thawed) raspberries
$^1/_2$ cup granulated sugar
1 $^1/_4$ cups milk
$^2/_3$ cup heavy cream
2 eggs
4 egg yolks
$^1/_4$ cup plus 1 tablespoon turbinado sugar* or light brown sugar

Preheat oven to 300° F. Butter six 6-ounce ramekins.

In a blender or food processor, puree the raspberries and granulated sugar. Strain to remove seeds. In a medium-sized saucepan, mix together the puree, milk, and cream and bring to a boil. In a medium-sized bowl, whisk together the eggs and egg yolks. Slowly add the hot milk mixture into the beaten eggs, stirring constantly.

Fill the prepared ramekins about three-fourths full and place in a baking pan. Add water to come halfway up the sides of the ramekins and bake for 30 to 35 minutes or until set. Let cool completely (preferably overnight in the refrigerator).

Preheat broiler. Sprinkle 1 $^1/_2$ tablespoons of the turbinado sugar evenly over the top of each ramekin and place the ramekins under the broiler until the sugar melts. Serve immediately.

Item is available in gourmet foods stores.

YIELD: 6 SERVINGS

Mountain Apple & Vidalia Onion Soup with Garlic Croutons

6 cups beef stock

3 1/2 cups apple cider

1 bay leaf

1 teaspoon dried thyme

1 teaspoon coarsely ground black pepper

3 tablespoons butter

5 medium Vidalia onions, thinly sliced

1 teaspoon salt

1 teaspoon granulated sugar

3/4 cup dry sherry

Toppings:

2 medium North Carolina red apples, unpeeled and finely diced

1/2 cup freshly grated Parmesan cheese

2 cups freshly grated Gruyère cheese

16 *Garlic Croutons* (see recipe below)

It is difficult to explain to the uninitiated what makes the Vidalia onion so special. Rather than attempting to explain, I encourage you to try this superb onion for yourself. Vidalia onions are a wonderfully sweet product, grown in Georgia and distributed almost everywhere in the U.S. in season. Also, there is an old-style variety of apple grown in the Blue Ridge Mountains known as "limber twig," which is the perfect cooking apple for this soup, but other varieties will work. This marriage of sweetness results in a soup that is simply divine.

In a large pot, combine the stock, 3 cups of the cider, the bay leaf, thyme, and black pepper and bring to a boil. Reduce heat to simmer and cook for 1 hour.

In a large skillet, melt the butter and sauté the onions for 3 minutes or until begin to wilt. Add the salt and sugar and continue to sauté until the onions are browned. Stir in the sherry to deglaze. When deglazed, add the onion mixture to the stock mixture and simmer for 1 hour more. Adjust the seasonings.

To make the toppings: In a small bowl, combine the apples and the remaining cider and set aside. In a separate bowl, mix together both cheeses and set aside.

Preheat broiler. Ladle the soup into ovenproof bowls and top each bowl with 2 Garlic Croutons. Cover with the cheese mixture and broil until nicely browned. Remove and top each with the diced apple mixture. Serve immediately.

YIELD: 8 SERVINGS

Garlic Croutons

1 baguette or loaf French bread, cut into $^{1}/_{2}$-inch slices
2 cloves garlic, peeled and halved
$^{1}/_{2}$ cup extra-virgin olive oil

Preheat oven to 350° F. Rub the bread slices with the cut garlic and place in a single layer on a rimmed baking sheet. Brush both sides of the bread with the oil and bake for 5 minutes or until golden and crisp.

White Chocolate & Cranberry Brownies

2 sticks butter, halved
4 ounces unsweetened chocolate, chopped
2 cups granulated sugar
4 eggs, beaten
$^{1}/_{4}$ teaspoon pure almond extract
$^{1}/_{2}$ teaspoon pure vanilla extract
1 cup all-purpose flour
1 cup chopped pecans
1 cup white chocolate chips
$^{1}/_{2}$ cup chopped dried cranberries

In a large saucepan, melt the butter and chocolate and stir in the sugar. Let cool to lukewarm.

Add the eggs to the chocolate mixture and mix together well. Stir in both extracts and the flour. In a small bowl, combine the pecans, chocolate chips, and cranberries and fold into the brownie mixture.

Preheat oven to 350° F. Pour the batter into a greased 9 x 13-inch baking pan and bake for about 30 minutes. Let cool on a wire rack. Cut and serve.

YIELD: 6 TO 8 SERVINGS

Chicken, Wild Rice & Peach Salad with Lime-Tarragon Dressing

Four 8-ounce chicken breasts, bone in
Salt and freshly ground black pepper to taste
1 teaspoon finely chopped fresh gingerroot
$^1/_2$ teaspoon fennel seeds
$^1/_2$ cup white wine

Salad:
3 cups cooked cooled wild rice
$^3/_4$ cup sliced toasted almonds (see box on page 21)
1 cup sliced celery
1 medium red bell pepper, seeded, deveined, and diced
$^1/_2$ teaspoon finely chopped fresh gingerroot
Salt and freshly ground black pepper to taste
1 recipe *Lime-Tarragon Dressing* (see recipe below)
2 cups peeled sliced fresh peaches, tossed with lemon juice
Fresh lettuce, rinsed and dried

In a large saucepan, place the chicken and cover with water. Add the salt, black pepper, ginger, fennel seeds, and wine and bring to a boil. Reduce heat to simmer and cook, covered, for 20 minutes, or until the chicken is cooked through. Let the chicken cool completely in the liquid.

When cold, reserve 2 tablespoons of the poaching liquid. Remove the skin from the chicken. Take the chicken off the bone and cut into pieces. Set aside.

To make the salad: In a large bowl, combine the reserved chicken, the wild rice, almonds, celery, bell pepper, and ginger. Add the salt and black pepper and toss with the *Lime-Tarragon Dressing*. Reserve some of the peach slices for garnish and gently mix the remaining peach slices into the chicken salad.

Place the salad on a bed of lettuce on each plate and fan a few peach slices out to the side. Serve immediately.

YIELD: 6 SERVINGS

Lime-Tarragon Dressing

1 cup mayonnaise
Grated zest of 1 lime
Juice of $^{1}/_{2}$ lime
1 teaspoon dried tarragon, or 2 teaspoons chopped fresh tarragon
2 tablespoons of the cooled poaching liquid
Salt and freshly ground black pepper to taste

In a small bowl, mix together the mayonnaise, zest, lime juice, and tarragon. Gradually add the poaching liquid, stirring until smooth. Add the salt and black pepper.

Grilled Scallops with Sunflower Seed-Basil Topping

1 recipe *Sunflower Seed-Basil Topping* (see recipe below)
24 large sea scallops
Juice of 1 lemon
$^1/_2$ cup olive oil
Salt and freshly ground white pepper to taste

Pat the scallops dry with paper towels. Thirty minutes before grilling, marinate the scallops in the lemon juice and oil for 20 minutes. Skewer the marinated scallops and season with the salt and white pepper.

Place the skewers directly over the hottest part of the grill. When tiny beads of moisture appear on the uncooked side of the scallops, turn the skewers and cook until the sides of the scallops are no longer translucent.

Arrange 3 scallops on each plate and top with the *Sunflower Seed-Basil Topping*. Serve immediately.

YIELD: 8 APPETIZER SERVINGS

Sunflower Seed-Basil Topping

$^1/_3$ cup olive oil
$^1/_2$ cup raw sunflower seeds
Freshly cracked black peppercorns
8 fresh basil leaves, rinsed and chopped

In a small skillet, heat the oil and sauté the seeds and cracked pepper until the seeds just begin to brown. Stir in the basil and sauté until the basil is crispy. Keep warm.

Lemon Risotto

3 tablespoons extra-virgin olive oil
1 leek, finely chopped (white part only)
1 shallot, finely chopped
2 cups uncooked arborio rice
$^1/_2$ cup dry white wine
Grated zest of 2 lemons
6 cups hot chicken stock
Salt and freshly ground white pepper to taste
2 tablespoons butter
1 cup freshly grated Parmesan cheese

In a large saucepan, heat the oil and sauté the leek and shallot for 3 to 5 minutes, or until the vegetables are tender. Add the rice and stir to coat with the oil. Mix in the wine and zest and stir until the wine is absorbed.

Add the hot stock to the rice, a ladleful at a time, stirring frequently. When the liquid has been absorbed, add more stock.

When the rice is cooked (firm but tender inside), add the salt, white pepper, and butter. Stir in the cheese and serve immediately.

YIELD: 8 SERVINGS

Sautéed Spinach with Mustard Seeds

1 tablespoon olive oil
1 tablespoon butter
2 tablespoons yellow mustard seeds
1 shallot, chopped
One 1-pound package fresh spinach, trimmed, rinsed, and dried
Salt and freshly ground black pepper to taste

In a large skillet, heat the oil and butter on medium heat and sauté the seeds and shallot until the seeds begin to pop. Add the spinach, salt, and black pepper and cook on high heat, stirring frequently, for 3 to 5 minutes. Serve immediately.

YIELD: 6 TO 8 SERVINGS

Remember when it was all you could do as a six year old to hold your nose and swallow your spinach without chewing it? Our more adult tastes have come about for a variety of reasons—primarily because talented chefs of the world have taught us the joys of seasoning and delicate preparation. The addition of mustard seeds to this sautéed spinach dish will forever erase those not-so-fond childhood memories of eating something just because it was good for you. Enjoy!

"Watermelon" Bombe

1 pint pistachio ice cream
1 pint lemon or vanilla ice cream
1 quart *Strawberry Sorbet* (see recipe below)
1 tablespoon chocolate chips

Line a 2-quart mold with plastic wrap. Press the pistachio ice cream around the mold and freeze until firm. Press the lemon ice cream over the pistachio layer and freeze until firm.

Scoop 1 pint of the *Strawberry Sorbet* into the mold, sprinkle with the chocolate chips, and cover with the remaining sorbet. Cover the mold and freeze until firm enough to slice.

To unmold the bombe, invert the mold onto a serving plate and peel off the plastic wrap. Smooth the surface with the tines of a fork. Serve immediately.

YIELD: VARIABLE SERVINGS

Strawberry Sorbet

1 cup granulated sugar
1 cup water
1 quart fresh ripe strawberries, rinsed and hulled
2 tablespoons vodka or Grand Marnier liqueur

To make sugar syrup: In a small saucepan, combine the sugar and water and cook on low heat, stirring constantly, until the sugar is dissolved. Bring to a boil. Turn off heat and let cool completely.

In a food processor, process the strawberries and $1/2$ cup of the cooled syrup until smooth. Strain to remove seeds. Add the strawberry mixture and vodka to the remaining syrup and mix together well. Freeze the sorbet in an ice-cream freezer according to the manufacturer's directions. Makes 1 quart.

Chapter 8

Crab Cakes with Poached Eggs & Potato Crisps

Rainbow Trout with Potato Scales

Bibb Lettuce with Orange Vinaigrette

Fruit Gazpacho

Lemon Granités

Goat Cheese Salad with Basil Vinaigrette & Mango Salsa

Rice Paper-Wrapped Yellowfin Tuna with Ginger Sauce

Lemon Beignets with Lemon-Buttermilk Sorbet & Berries

Mixed Grill with Red Wine Vinaigrette

Warm Apple Tarts with Applejack Sauce & Cinnamon Ice Cream

CHEF CORY MATTSON
The Fearrington House, Pittsboro, North Carolina

MICHAEL CUNNINGHAM

CHEF CORY MATTSON
The Fearrington House,
Pittsboro, North Carolina

The Fearrington House seems destined to earn every available distinction for excellence that exists in the industry. Chef Mattson, a Culinary Institute of America graduate has been instrumental in securing the only AAA 5-Diamond rating awarded to any restaurant or lodging establishment in North Carolina.

In addition to numerous pronouncements and awards designating it "The Best Inn" in recent years, The Fearrington House is one of the few Relais et Chateaux country inns in North America. The inn's popularity has been cited as one of the primary reasons for the successful creation of an entire European-style village on the grounds surrounding the inn.

Chef Mattson is a tireless leader who takes pride in overseeing a kitchen that has become a hallmark for country inn food and beverage excellence. In addition to participating in our series as one of the fourteen featured chefs, Cory served as Executive Chef of the entire production. In that role, he showed us why he is among the leaders of this business. He has chosen to set the height of the bar for others in this field and, in the process, to set the standards of excellence by which his peers are inevitably measured. Besides all of that, he is a superb cook!

Crab Cakes with Poached Eggs & Potato Crisps

10 ounces fresh crabmeat, cartilage removed

1 tablespoon chopped scallions

1 tablespoon chopped green bell pepper

1 tablespoon chopped celery

Salt and freshly ground black pepper to taste

$1/2$ beaten egg

$1/2$ teaspoon ground mustard

$1/2$ teaspoon mayonnaise

$1/4$ cup dried bread crumbs

1 tablespoon vegetable oil

Potato Crisps:

3 to 4 tablespoons clarified butter (see box on page 83)

4 Idaho potatoes, peeled, shredded, and divided

Poached Eggs:

$1/4$ cup white vinegar

4 cups water

4 eggs

> Leave it to Chef Mattson to turn breakfast into a culinary tour de force! This rich blending of crab cakes and eggs will probably change the way you look at breakfast from now on.

In a large bowl, mix together the crab, vegetables, salt, and black pepper. In a small bowl, stir together the egg, mustard, and mayonnaise. Add the egg mixture to the crab mixture and mix together well. Mix in the bread crumbs and and shape into 4 cakes.

In a large skillet, heat the oil and fry the cakes until brown on both sides and heated through. Keep warm.

To make the crisps: In a large skillet, heat the butter on medium heat and brown each shredded potato on both sides until crisp. Keep warm.

To make the eggs: In a large saucepan, combine the vinegar and water and bring to a simmer. Gently slide cracked eggs into the water and simmer for 3 minutes or cook until desired doneness.

Place 1 potato crisp on each plate and top with 1 crab cake. Place 1 poached egg on top of the crab cake and serve immediately.

YIELD: 4 SERVINGS

Rainbow Trout with Potato Scales

Cornstarch
Water
4 red new potatoes, very thinly sliced
Four 6-ounce fresh trout fillets, skinned
1/4 cup clarified butter (see box on page 83)
Salt and freshly ground black pepper to taste

In a small bowl, combine enough cornstarch and water to form a thin paste. Using the cornstarch mixture as "glue," layer the potatoes on skin side of the fillets, starting at the tail end and creating the effect of scales.

In a large skillet, heat the butter on medium heat. Add the fillets "scale"-side down and cook until golden brown on the edges. Flip and continue to cook until desired doneness. Season with the salt and black pepper. Remove and drain on paper towels. Place 1 fillet on each plate "scale"-side up and serve immediately.

YIELD: 4 SERVINGS

Bibb Lettuce with Orange Vinaigrette

1/3 cup cider vinegar
1 teaspoon honey
2 teaspoons orange syrup
Salt and freshly ground black pepper to taste
1 cup corn oil
Fresh Bibb lettuce, rinsed and dried
Almonds, sliced
Zest of 1 orange

In a blender or food processor, blend together the vinegar, honey, syrup, salt, and black pepper. While the blender is running, slowly add the oil and blend until smooth.

Serve the vinaigrette over the lettuce and garnish with the almonds and zest.

YIELD: 4 SERVINGS

Fruit Gazpacho

1 clove garlic, peeled
1 clove shallot, peeled
1 leek, well cleaned and coarsely chopped (white part only)
1 medium green bell pepper, seeded, deveined, and coarsely chopped
1 medium cucumber, coarsely chopped
$^1/_2$ medium red onion, coarsely chopped
4 scallions, coarsely chopped
1 fresh kiwifruit, peeled and sliced
$^1/_4$ cantaloupe, seeded and cubed
Juice of 1 lemon
Juice of 1 lime
1 cup V-8 juice
Salt and freshly ground black pepper to taste
Fresh cilantro, chopped

In a blender or food processor, mix together the first twelve ingredients until well combined. Season with the salt, black pepper, and cilantro. Chill for 30 minutes. Serve cold.

YIELD: 4 SERVINGS

Lemon Granités

$^1/_2$ cup fresh lemon juice
Granulated sugar to taste
$^1/_4$ teaspoon salt or to taste

In a small bowl, mix together all of the ingredients and strain into a hard-sided freezer container. Freeze until solid. Break up with a heavy fork and serve in small, glass dessert dishes.

YIELD: 4 SERVINGS

Goat Cheese Salad with Basil Vinaigrette & Mango Salsa

1 cup olive oil
1 sprig fresh thyme
1 sprig fresh rosemary
8 ounces goat cheese, cut with a wire into 4 medallions
1 cup dried bread crumbs
8 ounces fresh mixed baby greens
2 cups heated cooked black-eyed peas
1 recipe *Mango Salsa* (see recipe below)
1 recipe *Basil Vinaigrette* (see recipe below)

In a small bowl, combine the oil and herbs. Place the cheese medallions in a shallow glass baking dish and cover with the oil mixture. Let stand for at least 30 minutes.

Preheat oven to 350° F. Roll the marinated medallions in the bread crumbs. Place in a baking pan and bake for 5 minutes.

Divide the greens among the salad plates and place $1/2$ cup of the black-eyed peas on top of the greens. Divide the *Mango Salsa* on top of the peas and place 1 cheese medallion on top of the salsa. Spoon the *Basil Vinaigrette* around the greens and serve immediately.

Yield: 4 servings

Mango Salsa

1 medium apple, unpeeled and diced
1 medium red onion, diced
1 papaya, peeled and diced
1 mango, peeled and diced

In a medium-sized bowl, mix together all of the ingredients.

Basil Vinaigrette

1 cup chopped fresh basil
$^1/_3$ cup white wine vinegar
1 tablespoon honey
Salt and freshly ground white pepper to taste
$^3/_4$ cup plus 2 tablespoons olive oil

In a blender or food processor, blend together the first four ingredients. While the blender is running, add the oil and blend until smooth.

Rice Paper-Wrapped Yellowfin Tuna with Ginger Sauce

Four 6-ounce fresh yellowfin tuna steaks, trimmed
1 recipe *Ginger Sauce* (see recipe below)
1 egg, beaten
Vegetable oil

Cut each steak in half, but not all the way through the meat. Fold the two sections on top of each other and set aside.

For each steak, place one rice paper diagonally with corner facing you. Place a second rice paper on top of first paper with the bottom corner of the second paper overlapping the top corner of the first. The two papers should look like two diamonds intersecting. Brush the papers with the egg.

Place each steak in the center of its first paper and roll towards the second, wrapping in outside corners as you go. (The final product should resemble a large egg roll.)

In a large skillet, heat $^1/_4$ inch of the oil and fry the steaks until just golden brown. Drain and cut each roll into medallions with a serrated knife.

Divide the medallions among the plates and top with the *Ginger Sauce*. Serve immediately.

YIELD: 4 SERVINGS

Ginger Sauce

1 cup white wine
1 tablespoon honey
$^1/_2$ cup soy sauce
1 teaspoon dried red pepper flakes
1 tablespoon grated fresh gingerroot
1 to 2 tablespoons cornstarch dissolved in $^1/_4$ cup apple juice

In a small saucepan, combine the first five ingredients and bring to a simmer. Stir in the cornstarch mixture and cook, stirring frequently, until clear. Keep warm.

Lemon Beignets with Lemon-Buttermilk Sorbet & Berries

1 recipe *Lemon-Buttermilk Sorbet* (see recipe below)

Berry Mixture:
$^1/_2$ pint each: fresh blackberries, blueberries, and raspberries, rinsed
$^1/_2$ pint fresh strawberries, rinsed, hulled, and sliced
$^1/_2$ cup granulated sugar
2 to 3 tablespoons bottled raspberry or blackberry sauce
1 tablespoon Chambord liqueur

Beignets:
1 cup milk
Zest of 2 lemons, finely chopped
1 tablespoon granulated sugar
Pinch salt
$^1/_2$ cup (1 stick) butter
1 cup all-purpose flour
4 eggs
Vegetable oil

> Before you dismiss the idea of making homemade sorbet, you might want to give it a try! Save this recipe for that special, leisurely weekend brunch after you've slept a little later than usual. Cory's treatment of the old New Orleans favorite beignet has a zesty twist with a refreshing taste sensation. This may very well become your all-time favorite, summertime breakfast.

To make the berry mixture: In a large bowl, gently combine all of the ingredients and let stand for at least 30 minutes.

To make the beignets: In a heavy-bottomed saucepan, combine the milk, zest, sugar, salt, and butter and bring to a boil. Add the flour, stirring constantly, and cook until the mixture forms a ball and the saucepan bottom has a golden skin. Remove from heat and transfer to a separate bowl. Add the eggs, one at a time, beating after each addition, to make a smooth paste. Place the mixture in a pastry bag with a straight tip (Ateco #7).

In a large, deep skillet, heat 2 to 3 inches of the oil on medium-high heat. Pipe a small portion of the mixture onto a spoon (about the size of a walnut) and drop into the hot oil (350° F) and fry until golden. Drain on paper towels.

Place 10 to 12 beignets in each shallow dessert bowl and scoop the *Lemon-Buttermilk Sorbet* over the beignets. Ladle the berry mixture over all and serve immediately.

YIELD: 4 SERVINGS

Lemon-Buttermilk Sorbet

$^1/_2$ cup granulated sugar
$^1/_4$ cup water
2 cups buttermilk
$^1/_4$ cup fresh lemon juice

In a small saucepan, combine the sugar and water and bring to a boil. Reduce heat to medium-high and cook, stirring constantly, until the sugar dissolves. Let cool to room temperature.

In a medium-sized bowl, stir together $^3/_4$ cup of the cooled sugar mixture, the buttermilk, and lemon juice. Pour the mixture into an ice-cream maker and freeze according to manufacturer's directions.

Mixed Grill with Red Wine Vinaigrette

4 quails, deboned
4 veal medallions
4 lamb chops
1 Idaho potato
8 ounces fresh baby greens
1 recipe *Red Wine Vinaigrette* (see recipe below)
$^1/_2$ cup warm demi-glaze (rich brown sauce)

Grill the meats: quail for 2 minutes; veal for 3 minutes; and lamb for 4 minutes.

Meanwhile, cut the potato on a mandoline waffle-style and fry in a deep-fat frier until golden brown. Drain on paper towels.

In a medium-sized bowl, coat the greens with the *Red Wine Vinaigrette* and divide among the plates. Stand the fried potato slices in the greens and place the grilled meats around the greens and potatoes. Drizzle the demi-glaze over the top and serve immediately.

YIELD: 4 SERVINGS

Red Wine Vinaigrette

$^1/_3$ cup red wine vinegar
1 tablespoon red wine
1 teaspoon dried oregano
1 teaspoon dried thyme
1 tablespoon honey
Salt and freshly ground black pepper to taste
$^2/_3$ cup olive oil

In a blender or food processor, combine the first six ingredients. While the blender is running, slowly add the oil and blend until smooth.

Warm Apple Tarts with Applejack Sauce & Cinnamon Ice Cream

1 recipe *Cinnamon Ice Cream* (see recipe below)
8 ounces puff pastry sheets, thawed
1 recipe *Almond Cream* (see recipe below)
6 Granny Smith apples, peeled and thinly sliced
$^1/_2$ cup (1 stick) butter, divided
$^1/_2$ cup granulated sugar
1 recipe *Applejack Sauce* (see recipe below)

Preheat oven to 350° F. Cut out six 4 $^1/_2$-inch diameter circles from the pastry sheets (use a large cutter or a knife traced around a saucer). Spread each circle with 1 tablespoon *Almond Cream*.

Arrange the apple slices in a pinwheel fashion on the prepared pastry circles. Top with pats of the butter and sprinkle with the sugar. Place the tarts on a baking sheet and bake on the bottom rack of the oven for 30 minutes or until golden brown and baked on the bottom.

Generously coat the bottom of each dessert plate with the *Applejack Sauce*. Place 1 warm tart off center on each plate and scoop the *Cinnamon Ice Cream* on top. Serve immediately.

YIELD: 6 SERVINGS

Cinnamon Ice Cream

3 cups cream
1 cup milk
2 cinnamon sticks
8 egg yolks
1 cup granulated sugar
1 teaspoon ground cinnamon

In a heavy saucepan, combine the cream, milk, and cinnamon sticks and bring to a boil. Remove from heat and let stand for 15 minutes.

In a medium-sized bowl, whisk together the egg yolks, sugar, and ground cinnamon. Return the cream mixture to a boil. Add half of the boiling cream mixture to the egg yolk mixture and stir until well blended.

Return the combined mixture to the saucepan and cook on medium heat, stirring constantly, until the mixture coats the back of a spoon. Remove from heat and immediately strain into a separate container. Chill overnight.

Pour into an ice-cream maker and freeze according to manufacturer's directions.

Almond Cream

One 3 ¹/₂-ounce package sliced
  almonds, blanched
¹/₂ cup granulated sugar
¹/₄ cup (¹/₂ stick) butter
1 egg

1 egg yolk
Pinch salt
1 tablespoon rum
¹/₂ teaspoon pure vanilla extract

In a food processor, combine the almonds and sugar and process until the almonds are finely chopped, with a sandy appearance.

In a medium-sized bowl, cream together the butter and almond mixture with an electric mixer. Add the egg and egg yolk and beat together. Add the salt, rum, and vanilla and beat to a cookielike paste.

Applejack Sauce

1 cup granulated sugar
¹/₄ cup water
1 cup cream
3 tablespoons applejack brandy
¹/₄ cup (¹/₂ stick) butter

In a heavy saucepan, combine the sugar and water and bring to a boil. Continue to cook, without stirring, until the mixture turns the color of iced tea. Slowly add the cream and return to a boil. Remove from heat and stir in the brandy and butter. Keep warm.

Chapter 9

Soup of Collard Greens & Wild Rice with Hominy Crackers

Moon Pie

Blackberry Wine–Marinated Veal Chops
with Braised Ruby Chard
& White Bean & Sun–Dried Tomato Ragout

Yellow Tomato Gazpacho with Olivata Crouton

Cornmeal–Breaded Trout with Hominy Hash & Baked Eggs

Spiced Blackberry & Cornmeal Cobbler with Bourbon Sabayon

Spring Fool with Sesame Lace Cookies

CHEF JOHN FLEER
Inn at Blackberry Farm, Walland, Tennessee

COURTESY INN AT BLACKBERRY FARM

CHEF JOHN FLEER
Inn at Blackberry Farm,
Walland, Tennessee

This Four-Diamond country inn is one of only a handful of Relais & Chateaux inns in the United States, and Chef John Fleer is one of the big reasons why. Chef Fleer graduated from the highly regarded Culinary Institute of America in Hyde Park, New York, and quickly began accumulating an impressive dossier of experience at St. Andrews Cafe in Hyde Park and as the private chef of Mary Tyler Moore and her husband in their New York home.

John describes his cooking style as "foothills cuisine"—a style of food preparation and presentation that integrates the best of rugged/refined and classical/traditional techniques without compromising any one style. Chef Fleer drew his inspiration for foothills cuisine from other foothill landscapes and cultures around the world, such as Gascony, Alsace, and the Basque region. He describes a true gourmet dining experience as one that "reconnects us to our agricultural heritage and reminds us of the flavors and experiences of our past."

The foothills cuisine concept developed by Chef Fleer can be seen in every presentation from silver service breakfast in bed to Sunday Brunch, gourmet picnics, and four-course candlelit dinners at Blackberry Farm.

Soup of Collard Greens & Wild Rice with Hominy Crackers

1 recipe *Hominy Crackers* (see recipe below)
2 ounces good-quality bacon
³/₄ cups diced onions
¹/₄ cup diced celery
¹/₄ cup all-purpose flour
¹/₂ cup uncooked wild rice
8 cups chicken stock
3 ham hocks
8 cups sliced fresh collard greens
1 teaspoon chopped fresh thyme
1 bay leaf
Salt and freshly ground black pepper to taste
1 cup diced country ham

In a large pot, render the bacon and gently sauté the onions and celery. Add the flour and make a blond roux. Whisk in the stock. Add the ham hocks and rice and cook for 45 minutes.

In a large saucepan, blanch the collards in water, then add to the soup and cook for 15 minutes more. Stir in the thyme, bay leaf, salt, and black pepper. Poach the ham in the hot soup, then remove.

Ladle the soup into bowls and garnish with the diced ham. Serve immediately with the *Hominy Crackers*.

YIELD: 8 TO 10 SERVINGS

Hominy Crackers

1 cup all-purpose flour
¹/₂ teaspoon salt
2 teaspoons baking powder

1 tablespoon granulated sugar
$^1/_4$ teaspoon cayenne pepper
2 tablespoons vegetable shortening
$^1/_2$ cup cooked grits
3 tablespoons milk
1 tablespoon country ham scraps

Preheat oven to 350° F. Cover a baking sheet with parchment paper. In a medium-sized bowl, sift together the dry ingredients, then cut in the shortening. Stir in the grits, milk, and ham. Roll the mixture to $^1/_8$-inch thickness and cut into 3-inch long triangles. Place on prepared baking sheet and bake for 15 minutes or until lightly browned and crisp. Makes 30 crackers.

Moon Pie

1 recipe *Pistachio Brownie* (see recipe below)
Vanilla ice cream
1 recipe *Italian Meringue* (see recipe below)

Place 1 unganached *Pistachio Brownie* (with center cut out) on each plate and top with the ice cream. Add the ganached whole round of brownie and top with the *Italian Meringue*. If desired, place under the broiler to brown the top of meringue. Serve immediately.

YIELD: 6 TO 8 SERVINGS

Pistachio Brownie

8 ounces bittersweet chocolate
1 1/2 cups (3 sticks) butter
1/2 cup unsweetened cocoa powder
1 3/4 cups granulated sugar
3 eggs
1 tablespoon pure vanilla extract
3/4 cup all-purpose flour
1/2 cup chopped pistachio nuts
1/2 cup diced milk chocolate
1 recipe *Dark Chocolate Ganache* (see recipe below)

If you're from the south or know someone who is, you are probably already familiar with Moon Pies. Moon pies have been a southern traditional sweet treat for generations. Traditionally, the moon pie consists of two cookies filled with marshmallow filling then dipped in milk chocolate to cover the entire concoction. Let's just say the Blackberry Farm version is just a little bit different, but the results are every bit as delicious!

Line a jelly-roll pan with parchment paper cut to fit, then butter the paper.

Preheat oven to 375° F. In the top of a double boiler over simmering water, melt the bittersweet chocolate and butter. Sift in the cocoa and sugar. Remove from heat and stir until smooth. Whisk in the eggs and vanilla, then the flour, nuts, and milk chocolate. Pour the batter into the prepared pan and bake for 20 minutes or until just done.

Cut half of the brownies into rounds with a large round cutter. Cut remaining half into the same size, but with a small round removed from the center of each larger round. (This small, cut-out round will help hold the ice cream in place.) Spread the *Dark Chocolate Ganache* on each whole round (without center removed) and set aside.

Dark Chocolate Ganache

8 ounces dark chocolate, chopped
1 cup heavy cream

In a small bowl, place the chocolate. In a small saucepan, bring the cream to a boil. Pour the hot cream over the chocolate and stir until melted and fully blended.

Italian Meringue

1 cup granulated sugar
$^1/_4$ cup plus 2 tablespoons water
6 egg whites
$^1/_4$ teaspoon cream of tartar
6 tablespoons granulated sugar

In a small saucepan, combine the sugar and water and bring to a boil. Reduce heat and cook, stirring frequently, until the mixture reaches 245° F.

Meanwhile, in a medium-sized bowl, beat the egg whites and cream of tartar with an electric mixer until medium peaks form. Add the sugar and beat until medium-stiff peaks form.

When the sugar mixture reaches 245°, pour into a glass container to maintain temperature. Slowly add the sugar mixture to the beaten egg whites. When the sugar mixture is well blended, continue beating at medium speed for 5 minutes to cool.

Blackberry Wine-Marinated Veal Chops with Braised Ruby Chard & White Bean & Sun-Dried Tomato Ragout

Four 8-ounce farm-raised veal chops (Summerfield Farms, if available)
Salt and freshly ground black pepper to taste
1 recipe *Roasted Garlic & Shallot Jus* (see recipe below)
1 recipe *White Bean & Sun-Dried Tomato Ragout* (see recipe below)
1 recipe *Braised Ruby Chard* (see recipe below)
4 sprigs fresh rosemary, rinsed

Marinade:
1/4 cup chopped shallots
2 teaspoons chopped fresh rosemary
1 1/2 cups olive oil
3/4 cup blackberry wine

To make the marinade: In a medium-sized bowl, whisk together all of the ingredients. Place the chops in a shallow glass baking dish and marinate for 3 hours 30 minutes in the refrigerator. Remove the chops from the marinade and drain. Season with the salt and black pepper and grill to desired doneness.

Place 1 chop in the center of each plate and clockwise place the *White Bean & Sun-Dried Tomato Ragout, Roasted Garlic & Shallot Jus,* and on the other side of chop, place the *Braised Ruby Chard.* Serve immediately.
YIELD: 4 SERVINGS

Roasted Garlic & Shallot Jus

1 head garlic, unpeeled and separated into cloves
2 tablespoons olive oil

12 shallots, peeled
1 1/2 cups veal stock
1/2 cup blackberry wine

Preheat oven to 300° F. In a small ovenproof skillet, toss the unpeeled garlic cloves in 1 tablespoon of the oil, cover, and bake for 35 to 40 minutes or until tender. Peel the garlic and set aside.

In the same skillet, heat the remaining oil on medium-high heat and sear the shallots. Increase oven temperature to 400° and bake the shallots until tender, about 10 minutes.

In a sauté pan, warm the garlic and shallots. Add the wine and deglaze the pan. Add the stock and reduce slightly.

White Bean & Sun-Dried Tomato Ragout

1 tablespoon vegetable oil
¼ cup diced country ham
½ cup diced onions
¼ cup diced carrots
¼ cup diced celery
4 cups chicken stock

8 ounces dried white beans
Pinch cayenne pepper
Pinch crushed dried red pepper flakes
Salt and freshly ground black pepper to taste
½ cup julienned sun-dried tomatoes

In a large saucepan, heat the oil and sauté the ham until golden brown. Add the onions and sauté for 3 to 5 minutes. Add the carrots and celery and sauté for 5 to 8 minutes. Stir in the stock, beans, and seasonings and simmer for 30 to 45 minutes, or until the beans are tender. Add the tomatoes and let rehydrate in the liquid before serving.

Braised Ruby Chard

1 tablespoon olive oil
2 bunches fresh ruby chard, cleaned and stemmed; reserve stems
1 tablespoon chopped shallot
Salt and freshly ground black pepper to taste
2 tablespoons chicken stock

Heat a large sauté pan on medium-high heat and add the oil. Dice the reserved chard stems and add to the pan. Stir in the shallot, chard leaves, salt, and black pepper and cook for 3 to 4 minutes. Deglaze the pan with the stock. Turn the mixture over, cover, and turn off heat. Let stand for 5 to 10 seconds.

Yellow Tomato Gazpacho with Olivata Crouton

1 recipe *Olivata Crouton* (see recipe below)
2 pounds fresh ripe yellow tomatoes, chopped, not seeded
1 medium yellow bell pepper, seeded, deveined, and large diced
$^1/_2$ medium zucchini, peeled, seeded, and chopped
1 medium cucumber, peeled, seeded, and chopped
$^1/_4$ teaspoon finely chopped garlic
$^1/_4$ cup chopped Vidalia onions
$^3/_4$ teaspoon Worcestershire sauce
$^1/_2$ tablespoon hot sauce
$^1/_4$ cup white wine
2 tablespoons rice vinegar
2 tablespoons fresh lime juice
Salt and freshly cracked black peppercorns to taste

Garnish:
Cucumbers, peeled and diced
Cooked corn kernels, at room temperature
Red and yellow fresh tomatoes, chopped
Limes, diced
Fresh herbs, finely chopped (chives, tarragon, parsley)
Green onions, cut on bias

In a blender or food processor, puree the first twelve ingredients and strain through a small-mesh strainer (not fine-mesh). Chill. Adjust the seasonings.

To make the garnish: Prepare all of the ingredients and place in separate bowls.

Ladle the gazpacho into chilled bowls and garnish each with the cucumbers, corn, tomatoes, and limes. Top with the herbs and green onions. Serve cold with the *Olivata Crouton.*

YIELD: 8 TO 10 SERVINGS

Olivata Crouton

1 cup pitted calamata olives
$1/2$ cup sun-dried tomatoes, rehydrated (see box on page 76)
$1/2$ tablespoon extra-virgin olive oil
1 teaspoon chopped garlic
2 tablespoons fresh basil leaves
$1/8$ teaspoon salt
$1/4$ teaspoon freshly cracked black peppercorns
One 16-inch baguette of French bread, cut into $1/4$-inch thick slices

In a food processor, combine all of the ingredients, except the bread, and blend to a smooth paste. Scrape down the sides and process again briefly. Spread the mixture on the bread slices and serve with the gazpacho.

Cornmeal-Breaded Trout with Hominy Hash & Baked Eggs

1 recipe *Hominy Hash* (see recipe below)
Ten 8-ounce fresh trout, dressed
Salt and freshly cracked black peppercorns
2 cups buttermilk
1 tablespoon Tabasco sauce
2 cups cornmeal
2 cups all-purpose flour
$1/4$ cup Old Bay Seasoning
2 tablespoons onion powder
$1/4$ cup clarified butter (see box on page 83)
1 recipe *Baked Eggs* (see recipe below)
1 bunch fresh watercress, rinsed and dried

> This is Chef Fleer's foothills cuisine at its finest. Intelligent balance, superb plate presentation, and unforgettably delicious are the hallmarks of this wonderful dish.

To prepare the trout: Remove the head and fatty trim from both sides of the belly. Season the inside of each trout with the salt and cracked pepper. In a medium-sized bowl, combine the buttermilk and Tabasco sauce. Dip each trout in the buttermilk mixture and wipe off excess. In another bowl, mix together the cornmeal, flour, Old Bay Seasoning, and onion powder. Dredge each trout in the cornmeal mixture and shake off excess.

Preheat oven to 375° F. In a large ovenproof skillet, heat the butter on medium-high heat and brown both sides of the trout. Place the trout in the oven and bake for about 7 minutes to finish cooking.

Place 1 trout at the back of each plate. Stuff the inside of each trout with the *Hominy Hash* and place the *Baked Eggs* next to the tail. Place a small mound of the watercress on the side of the eggs and serve immediately.

YIELD: 10 SERVINGS

Hominy Hash

2 to 3 tablespoons vegetable oil
$1/2$ cup diced celery
$1/2$ cup diced onions
$1/2$ cup diced red bell peppers
$1/2$ cup diced green bell peppers
1 tablespoon finely diced jalapeño pepper
1 tablespoon chopped green onions
1 teaspoon salt
1 teaspoon freshly cracked black peppercorns
$1/2$ cup cooked diced country ham
3 cups cooked diced potatoes
3 cups cooked hominy
$1/2$ tablespoon chopped fresh chives
$1/2$ tablespoon chopped fresh parsley

In a large, deep skillet, heat the oil and sauté the next six ingredients for 4 to 6 minutes or until tender. Add the salt and cracked pepper. Stir in the ham, potatoes, and hominy and cook until heated through. Add the herbs and keep warm.

Baked Eggs

20 eggs
$1/2$ cup grated smoked Gouda cheese
1 bunch green onions, cut on bias

Spray 10 ramekins with cooking spray and break 2 eggs into each ramekin. Place the ramekins in a steamer and steam for 5 minutes or until the outsides of the eggs are set. (Yolks should still be quite runny.)

Remove and sprinkle each ramekin with 1 tablespoon of the cheese. Place the ramekins under the broiler and broil until the cheese melts. Sprinkle with the greens onions and serve immediately.

Spiced Blackberry & Cornmeal Cobbler with Bourbon Sabayon

1 ¹/₂ cups granulated sugar
¹/₄ cup packed brown sugar
¹/₂ tablespoon finely chopped lemon zest
1 teaspoon ground cinnamon
1 teaspoon ground nutmeg
1 ¹/₂ tablespoons cornstarch
1 tablespoon dark rum
6 cups fresh blackberries, rinsed
1 recipe *Bourbon Sabayon* (see recipe below)

Topping:
1 ¹/₄ sticks butter, softened
1 ¹/₂ cups confectioners' sugar
3 eggs, beaten
1 ¹/₂ cups all-purpose flour
1 ¹/₂ cups corn flour (Masa Harina)
1 cup cornmeal
1 tablespoon baking powder
³/₄ teaspoon baking soda
¹/₂ teaspoon ground cloves
2 ¹/₄ cups buttermilk

In a large bowl, combine the first seven ingredients. Fold in the blackberries and toss to coat. Place the mixture in a lightly greased 9 x 13-inch baking pan and set aside.

To make the topping: In a large bowl, cream together the butter and sugar. Stir in the eggs and cream until well combined. In a separate bowl, combine both flours, the cornmeal, baking powder, baking soda, and cloves. Add the flour mixture to the butter mixture, alternating with the buttermilk, and mix together well.

Preheat oven to 350° F. Place the batter in a pastry bag with straight tip and pipe the batter onto the reserved blackberries in a trellis pattern. Bake for 35 to 45 minutes, or until the crust is browned and the fruit is bubbly. Let cool on a wire rack. Serve topped with the *Bourbon Sabayon*.

YIELD: 8 TO 10 SERVINGS

Bourbon Sabayon

8 egg yolks
1 cup granulated sugar
$^1/_2$ cup plus 2 tablespoons bourbon whiskey
4 cups heavy cream

In a large stainless steel bowl, beat together the egg yolks and sugar until well blended. Add the whiskey and cook the mixture over a hot water bath, whipping constantly until thick and pale yellow. Chill.

In another bowl, whip the cream until very soft peaks form, then fold into the chilled bourbon mixture. Chill.

Spring Fool with Sesame Lace Cookies

1 recipe *Sesame Lace Cookies* (see
  recipe below)
1 cup chopped fresh rhubarb
$^1/_2$ cup granulated sugar
$^1/_2$ cup water

1 $^1/_2$ cups strawberries, rinsed, hulled,
  and halved
1 cup heavy cream
1 tablespoon brown sugar
Fresh small strawberries, rinsed

In a large saucepan, combine the rhubarb, granulated sugar, and water and cook on medium heat for 10 to 15 minutes, or until the rhubarb is very tender.

Increase heat to medium-high and cook, stirring frequently, until the mixture becomes syrupy. Immediately toss in the 1 $^1/_2$ cups strawberries. Remove from heat, cover, and let stand for 15 minutes. Strain through a sieve and let cool.

In a small bowl, whip the cream with the brown sugar until soft, firm peaks form. Fold the whipped cream into the cooled rhubarb mixture and pour into champagne flutes or ice-cream dishes. Garnish with the small strawberries and the *Sesame Lace Cookies*. Serve immediately.

YIELD: 6 SERVINGS

Sesame Lace Cookies

1 $^1/_4$ sticks butter
$^1/_2$ cup plus 2 tablespoons light corn
  syrup
1 cup packed brown sugar

1 tablespoon sesame oil
$^3/_4$ cup all-purpose flour
$^1/_4$ cup white sesame seeds
1 tablespoon black sesame seeds

In a large saucepan, combine the butter, corn syrup, brown sugar, and sesame oil and bring to a boil. Remove from heat and stir in the flour and all of the sesame seeds. Pour the batter into a baking pan and let cool.

Preheat oven to 375° F. Scoop the cooled batter onto baking sheets (6 per sheet) and bake for 9 minutes or until the bubbling stops. Let cool *slightly* and lift off baking sheet. Place each cookie over desired mold (small glass or muffin cup) and let cool completely. Makes 2 dozen.

Chapter 10

Clams with Tomatoes, Okra & Chorizo

Baked Red Snapper with Chèvre Cream Sauce
& Caramelized Vidalias

Peach & Blackberry Cobbler

Seared Cobia with Tomato Concassé

Chocolate Ganache Tart with Pecan Crust

Tuna Loin with Brown Sugar-Tamari Glaze

Baked Spicy Flounder with Mustard Greens & Sweet Potatoes

Grilled Scallops with Roasted Red Pepper Vinaigrette

Grilled Grouper with Saffron-Habanero Risotto

CHEF SHELLEY WALKER
Greyfield Inn, Cumberland Island, Georgia

COURTESY GREYFIELD INN

CHEF SHELLEY WALKER
Greyfield Inn, Cumberland Island, Georgia

Chef Walker may very well be the quintessential renaissance man when it comes to country inn cooking. He has spent more than a decade learning his craft from highly regarded executive chefs in Dallas, San Francisco, and Atlanta. Since 1993, Shelley has been able to quite successfully combine his love of the outdoors with his passion for uniquely prepared dishes.

If Chef Walker is not in the kitchen preparing one of his wonderfully fresh seafood creations, you will likely find him stalking shrimp in the shallows with his drift net or deftly casting for one of the trophy trout or redfish that abound near the island.

Cumberland Island, once the exclusive haunt of millionaires and their families, is now a reasonably accessible barrier island off the Georgia coast that is reached by only a fortunate few who travel via launch from Fernandina Beach, Florida. As you approach the peaceful moss-shrouded harbor and dock that serves the historic Greyfield Inn, it is immediately clear why Shelley does what he does where he does it!

Clams with Tomatoes, Okra & Chorizo

³/₄ cup clarified butter (see box on page 83)
1 cup chopped chorizo sausage
8 cloves garlic, chopped
32 fresh clams in shell
20 medium fresh okra, trimmed
6 cups chicken stock
2 cups white wine
12 fresh Italian plum tomatoes, peeled, seeded and chopped
Salt and freshly ground black pepper to taste

In a large saucepan, heat the butter and cook the sausage and garlic on medium heat until the fat begins to release from the sausage.

Increase heat to high, add the clams and okra, and sauté for 1 to 2 minutes, gently stirring once or twice. Drain off fat. Stir in the stock and wine and deglaze the saucepan. Add the tomatoes, salt, and black pepper and cook until the tomatoes are heated through.

Divide the mixture among 4 bowls and serve immediately.

YIELD: 4 APPETIZER SERVINGS

Baked Red Snapper with Chèvre Cream Sauce & Caramelized Vidalias

1 recipe *Chèvre Cream Sauce* (see recipe below)
2 tablespoons olive oil or more
Four 14- to 16-ounce fresh red snapper fillets with skin
1/4 cup clarified butter (see box on page 83)
8 medium Vidalia onions, halved and sliced
4 tablespoons chopped fresh chives

Preheat oven to 400° F. In a large skillet, heat the oil on high heat and sear each fillet on each side for 1 to 2 minutes. Place the fillets in a baking pan and bake for 15 to 20 minutes or until the fish flakes. In a large sauté pan, heat the butter and sauté the onions until golden brown and caramelized.

Ladle 1/4 cup *Chèvre Cream Sauce* on each plate and place 1 fillet on the sauce and the caramelized onions on top of each fillet. Sprinkle 1 tablespoon of the chives on each fillet and serve immediately.

YIELD: 4 SERVINGS

Chèvre Cream Sauce

2 cups heavy cream
8 ounces chèvre cheese
Zest of 8 lemons
Salt and freshly cracked white
  peppercorms to taste

In a medium-sized saucepan, reduce the cream on medium-high heat by half. Reduce heat to medium and add the cheese, zest, salt, and cracked pepper, stirring constantly, until the cheese is melted. Keep warm.

Shelley's rendition of this dish takes on a uniquely south Georgia look, aroma, and taste when the *Chèvre Cream Sauce* is in perfect harmony with the caramelized Vidalia onions. As we watched him work in the studio kitchen, we saw the same contrasts in the man. He had the appearance of a ruddy sun-tanned fisherman until he began working with the tools of the trade. His skills with a fishing rod are nicely balanced with a solid grasp of the basics of his business.

Peach & Blackberry Cobbler

3 cups peeled sliced fresh peaches
4 pints fresh blackberries
1 cup granulated sugar
2 tablespoons fresh lemon juice
2 cups unbleached all-purpose flour
1 tablespoon baking powder
$1/3$ cup butter
1 egg
$1/3$ cup milk
2 tablespoons granulated sugar

In a large bowl, combine the peaches, blackberries, $1/2$ cup of the sugar, and the lemon juice. Set aside.

In another bowl, mix together the remaining $1/2$ cup sugar, the flour, and baking powder and cut in the butter. In a small bowl, beat together the egg and milk and stir into the flour mixture to form a smooth dough.

Preheat oven to 425° F. In a deep baking dish, spread the reserved peach mixture. Pull off small pieces of the dough, press to flatten, and cover the peach mixture with the flatten dough.

Sprinkle the top with the 2 tablespoons sugar and bake for 30 to 40 minutes or until lightly browned on top. Let cool on a wire rack or serve warm.

YIELD: 6 TO 8 SERVINGS

Seared Cobia with Tomato Concassé

3 tablespoons olive oil or more
Four 6-ounce fresh cobia (shark) fillets
2 cups white wine
8 cloves garlic, finely chopped
2 cups fresh Roma tomatoes, peeled, seeded, and diced
1 to 2 tablespoons olive oil
20 medium fresh shiitake mushrooms, cleaned and trimmed
12 bunches fresh baby spinach, rinsed and trimmed
Salt and freshly ground black pepper to taste
4 lemons, halved
4 bunches fresh watercress, rinsed and dried

In a large skillet, heat the oil on high heat and sear each fillet on both sides for 3 to 5 minutes total, depending on thickness of fillet. Add more oil if needed and repeat procedure with remaining fillets. Remove from skillet and keep warm.

Drain excess oil from the skillet and deglaze with the wine. Stir in the garlic and tomatoes and cook for 3 to 5 minutes. Remove from heat and keep warm.

In a large saucepan, heat the 1 to 2 tablespoons oil and sauté the mushrooms until tender. Add the spinach and cover for 5 minutes. Remove from heat and add the salt and black pepper. Squeeze the lemon halves over the spinach mixture.

Divide the spinach mixture among the plates and place 1 fillet on top of the spinach. Top each fillet with the tomato concassé and serve immediately.

YIELD: 4 SERVINGS

Chocolate Ganache Tart with Pecan Crust

Crust:
6 ounces whole pecans
$1/2$ cup granulated sugar
3 tablespoons softened butter

Filling:
10 ounces bittersweet chocolate
1 cup heavy cream
$1/3$ cup sour cream
1 egg yolk
2 ounces semisweet chocolate
2 tablespoons Kahlua liqueur
$1/3$ cup granulated sugar
12 toasted whole pecans

Preheat oven to 350° F. To make the crust: In a food processor, chop the pecans. Add the sugar and process to combine. Add the butter and process until the mixture sticks together. Press the dough into a 9-inch tart pan and bake for 15 to 20 minutes or until golden brown. Let cool on a wire rack.

To make the filling: In a double boiler over simmering water, melt the bittersweet chocolate, stirring until smooth. In another saucepan, whisk together the cream, sour cream, and egg yolk on medium heat until hot. (Do not let the mixture bubble or the egg will curdle.) Add the semisweet chocolate and liqueur and remove from heat. Stir the melted bittersweet chocolate and sugar into the cream mixture until well blended.

Pour the mixture into the cooled crust and chill for 4 hours. Remove from the refrigerator 30 minutes before serving. Garnish with the whole pecans and serve.

YIELD: 6 TO 8 SERVINGS

Tuna Loin with Brown Sugar-Tamari Glaze

2 tablespoons olive oil

Four 2-ounce fresh tuna loins

$1/2$ cup sake wine

4 tablespoons finely chopped fresh gingerroot

$1/2$ cup packed brown sugar

1 cup tamari soy sauce

2 teaspoons red chili oil*

1 cup fresh mung bean sprouts

2 small cucumbers, peeled, seeded, and diced

4 green onions, finely chopped

1 tablespoon rice vinegar

Wasabi sauce*

Pickled ginger*

Fresh enoki mushrooms, rinsed and trimmed

Sesame seeds

> This is a terrific example of the fusion of tastes and cuisine that you've been hearing so much about. The brown sugar and tamari successfully marry the Pacific Rim and Southeast U.S. in a manner that would make any hard-fighting tuna proud.

In a large skillet, heat the olive oil on high and sear the loins for 2 to 3 minutes on each side or until rare and almost dark. Remove from heat and keep warm.

In a medium-sized saucepan, heat the wine. Add the ginger, sugar, and chili oil, stirring to dissolve the sugar. Mix in the tamari and remove from heat.

Glaze the loins with the tamari mixture. In a medium-sized bowl, toss together the sprouts, cucumbers, green onions, and vinegar.

Place $1/4$ cup sprout salad in the center of each plate. Place 1 loin on top of the sprouts and garnish with the wasabi sauce, pickled ginger, enoki mushrooms, and sesame seeds. Serve immediately.

*Items are available in natural foods stores.

YIELD: 4 APPETIZER SERVINGS

Baked Spicy Flounder with Mustard Greens & Sweet Potatoes

Juice of 4 limes
4 teaspoons finely ground sea salt
4 serrano chili peppers, finely chopped
Four 14- to 16-ounce fresh flounder fillets
2 to 3 tablespoons olive oil
4 medium bunches fresh mustard greens, rinsed, trimmed,
    and cut into $1/4$-inch strips
4 medium sweet potatoes, blanched and diced
8 cloves garlic, finely chopped
4 cups white wine

Preheat oven to 400° F. In a small bowl, mix together the lime juice, salt, and chili peppers. Score the skin of the flounders in a crosshatch pattern and rub with the chili pepper mixture. Place the flounders in a baking pan and bake for 15 to 20 minutes, or until the fish flakes.

In a large skillet, heat the oil on high heat and sauté the greens for 2 minutes. Stir in the potatoes and garlic. Add the wine, cover, and steam for 4 to 5 minutes, or until the greens are wilted and the potatoes are tender.

Place 1 flounder on each plate and a small amount of the greens slightly over and at the side of the flounder. Sprinkle the potatoes and garlic around the flounder and serve immediately.

YIELD: 4 SERVINGS

Grilled Scallops with Roasted Red Pepper Vinaigrette

12 baby artichokes, rinsed and trimmed
4 roasted medium red bell peppers, seeded, deveined, and diced
$^{1}/_{2}$ cup balsamic vinegar
$^{1}/_{2}$ cup olive oil
4 cloves garlic, finely chopped
Salt and freshly ground black pepper to taste
16 sprigs fresh thyme, rinsed
12 fresh sea scallops
16 calamata olives
Fresh basil, chopped

Steam the artichokes for 30 to 35 minutes. Set aside. In a medium-sized bowl, whisk together the bell peppers, vinegar, oil, garlic, salt, and black pepper. Stir in the thyme.

Place the scallops on a hot, oiled broiler pan and grill for 1 $^{1}/_{2}$ minutes on each side.

Ladle $^{1}/_{4}$ cup of the vinaigrette on each plate and arrange on each plate 3 scallops, 3 artichokes, and 4 olives. Garnish with the basil and serve immediately.

YIELD: 4 APPETIZER SERVINGS

Grilled Grouper with Saffron-Habanero Risotto

2 tablespoons clarified butter (see box on page 83)
4 medium onions, chopped
$1/2$ teaspoon saffron threads
1 habanero chili pepper, finely chopped
2 cups uncooked arborio rice
10 cups chicken stock
Salt to taste
Four 6-ounce fresh grouper fillets
Fresh chives, chopped
12 whole cloves elephant garlic, blanched and very thinly sliced
Olive oil

In a large saucepan, heat the butter and sauté the onions and saffron for 3 to 5 minutes. Add the chili pepper. Slowly stir in the rice, then slowly add the stock just until moistened. Cook slowly, stirring constantly, and adding more stock as the liquid is absorbed. Cook for 20 minutes, or until the rice is creamy and tender. Add the salt and keep warm.

Place the fillets on a hot, oiled broiler pan and grill for 4 minutes on each side.

Place each fillet on a bed of the risotto. Garnish with the chives and garlic and drizzle with the oil. Serve immediately.

YIELD: 4 SERVINGS

Chapter 11

Pumpkin Bisque with Maine Crabmeat & Cinnamon Croutons

Hazelnut Meringue with Pâte à Choux Nets
& Kahlua Chocolate Sauce

Sautéed Pork Loin with Julienned Vegetables
& Apple-Cinnamon Sauce

Chocolate Bourbon Pecan Tart

Sautéed Shrimp with Endive, Leeks & Pernod Sauce

Roasted Lamb Loin with Black Bean, Corn & Mango Salsa

Roasted Anjou Pears with Blackberry Sauce
& Stilton Blue Cheese Quenelles

Jalapeño & Roasted Corn Soup

Tuna Loin Wrapped in Pancétta with Gazpacho,
Roasted Parmesan & Sun-Dried Tomato Polenta

CHEF DOUG ALLEY
Josephine's Bed & Breakfast, Seaside, Florida

DAVID SHEA

CHEF DOUG ALLEY
Josephine's Bed & Breakfast,
Seaside, Florida

The French country inn where Chef Alley most recently hangs his toque is a new inn in a town created to reflect the best of everything old. Seaside, Florida, in the panhandle near Pensacola is a developers' dream come true. The gentle turquoise waters of the gulf of Mexico lap rhythmically across the pristine white sand of one of America's most unusual planned communities.

Pastel-colored, Florida-style homes cluster together within walking (or golf cart) distance of all of the infrastructure and services needed to make any town run, including a beautiful little inn. Josephine's, due in great measure to the fast-rising reputation of Doug Alley, has established itself as one of the area's finest dining establishments.

Chef Alley is one of the new garde of young innovative chefs who takes great pride in setting the standards by which many of his peers are measured. He began his colorful, award-winning career in 1987 as a member of the first USA student culinary team. His love of simple, elegant foods and his desire to excel in his profession quickly earned him an array of domestic and international culinary distinctions.

On the set of the "Inn Country Chefs" television series, Doug quickly impressed the crew with his professionalism and good humor. His cheerful disposition and ever-present smile have quickly become hallmarks of his kitchen demeanor.

Pumpkin Bisque with Maine Crabmeat & Cinnamon Croutons

2 tablespoons butter

2 pounds cleaned fresh pumpkin*

1 cup chopped Vidalia onions

2 tablespoons chopped garlic

3 cups chicken stock

$^1/_2$ teaspoon salt

$^1/_2$ teaspoon freshly ground black pepper

$^1/_2$ cup packed brown sugar

$^1/_2$ teaspoon ground nutmeg

$^1/_2$ teaspoon ground cloves

$^1/_2$ teaspoon ground ginger

$^1/_2$ teaspoon ground cinnamon

$^3/_4$ cup heavy cream

1 recipe *Cinnamon Croutons* (see recipe below)

2 cups cooked shredded Maine crabmeat

Like a lot of the recipes that you'll discover in this collection, this unusual combination of rich pumpkin bisque and lump crabmeat is elevated to "star status" by the light and sensational final touch. When cinnamon is introduced to the croutons in this recipe, you may feel you are boldly going where no one has gone before, but fear not. The cinnamon croutons are sure to be a hit with your guests!

In a large pot, melt the butter and sauté the pumpkin, onions, and garlic for 4 to 6 minutes, or until the pumpkin is tender. Deglaze the pot with the stock. Add the salt, black pepper, sugar, nutmeg, cloves, ginger, and cinnamon and simmer slowly until the pumpkin is fully cooked. Remove from heat.

In a blender or food processor, puree the bisque in batches. Return to the pot and slowly whisk in the cream. Keep warm.

Ladle the bisque into bowls and place 2 *Cinnamon Croutons* on top. Garnish with the crabmeat and serve immediately.

*Three 15 $^1/_2$-ounce cans pumpkin may be substituted for the fresh pumpkin.

YIELD: 8 TO 10 SERVINGS

Cinnamon Croutons

1 loaf French bread, cubed
$^1/_2$ cup (1 stick) butter, divided
1 tablespoon ground cinnamon
1 tablespoon granulated sugar

Preheat oven to 325° F. In a medium-sized bowl, toss together the bread cubes, butter, cinnamon, and sugar until evenly coated. Spread on a baking sheet and toast in the oven until crispy.

Hazelnut Meringue with Pâte à Choux Nets & Kahlua Chocolate Sauce

1 ¹/₂ cups ground hazelnuts
1 ¹/₂ cups granulated sugar
6 egg whites
¹/₂ teaspoon cream of tartar
1 recipe *Pâte à Choux Nets* (see recipe below)
1 recipe *Kahlua Chocolate Sauce* (see recipe below)
Frozen vanilla yogurt
Confectioners' sugar

Cover a baking sheet with parchment paper. In a small bowl, combine the hazelnuts and sugar. In a large bowl, beat the egg whites with an electric mixer until soft peaks form. Gently fold the sugar mixture into the egg mixture. (Do not overwork the meringue.)

Preheat oven to 200° F. Spoon the meringue into a pastry bag with star tip until half full. Hold the bag a half inch above the prepared baking sheet and with the tip pointing straight down, press the bag until desired size is formed (make 12 meringues). Bake for 45 minutes or until lightly golden brown.

Gently collapse the bottom of the meringues and fill with the frozen yogurt. Ladle ¹/₄ cup *Kahlua Chocolate Sauce* in the center of each plate until the surface is covered. Place 3 meringues in the center of each plate. Dust 3 *Pâte à Choux Nets* with the confectioners' sugar and gently place 1 net on each meringue, leaning toward the center of the plate. Serve immediately.

YIELD: 4 SERVINGS

Pâte à Choux Nets

1 ¹/₂ cups all-purpose flour
1 egg
¹/₈ teaspoon salt

Cover a baking sheet with parchment paper. In a medium-sized bowl, stir together all of the ingredients until a firm paste is formed. Let stand for 10 minutes.

Preheat oven to 375° F. Fill the pastry bag with the mixture. Pipe out crisscross patterns, resembling small nets, on the prepared baking sheet (make 12 nets) and bake for 15 minutes or until golden brown.

Kahlua Chocolate Sauce

1 tablespoon water
3 tablespoons Kahlua liqueur
3 tablespoons granulated sugar
$^3/_4$ cup crumbled semisweet chocolate
$^1/_4$ cup unsweetened chocolate
1 cup whipping cream

In a small saucepan, combine the water, liqueur, and sugar and bring to a boil on low heat, stirring constantly until the sugar dissolves. Remove from heat and let cool.

In the top of a double boiler over hot water, melt both chocolates, stirring until smooth. Remove from heat and stir in the cooled sugar mixture until smooth and well blended.

In a medium-sized saucepan, heat the cream on low heat until reaches 120° F. Pour in the chocolate mixture and stir until smooth and shiny.

Sautéed Pork Loin with Julienned Vegetables & Apple-Cinnamon Sauce

1 clove garlic, finely chopped
$^1/_2$ teaspoon salt
$^1/_2$ teaspoon freshly ground black
  pepper
1 tablespoon Dijon mustard
2 pounds pork loin, trimmed
Flour
1 tablespoon butter

Vegetables:
2 tablespoons butter
$^1/_4$ cup finely julienned and blanched
  leeks
$^1/_4$ cup finely julienned and blanched
  carrots
$^1/_4$ cup finely julienned napa cabbage
$^1/_4$ cup finely julienned jícama
$^1/_4$ cup finely julienned unpeeled apples
$^1/_4$ teaspoon salt
$^1/_4$ teaspoon freshly ground black
  pepper
2 tablespoons white wine
2 tablespoons apple cider

Sauce:
$^1/_4$ cup applejack brandy
$^1/_2$ cup apple cider
1 teaspoon ground cinnamon
$^1/_4$ teaspoon salt
2 tablespoons cold butter

In a small bowl, combine the garlic, salt, black pepper, and mustard and evenly coat the loin with the mixture. Let stand for 1 hour. Cut the loin evenly into 20 slices and set aside.

To make the vegetables: In a medium-sized skillet, melt the butter and sauté the vegetables, fruit, salt, and black pepper for 5 to 8 minutes, or until the vegetables are tender. Deglaze the skillet with the wine and cider and reduce by half.

Preheat oven to 375° F. Dredge the reserved pork slices in the flour. In a large skillet, melt the butter and brown the pork on each side. Place the slices in a baking pan and bake for 5 to 8 minutes.

To make the sauce: Deglaze the skillet with the brandy. Add the remaining ingredients, except the cold butter, and reduce by half. Remove from heat and whisk in the cold butter.

Arrange 5 slices of the pork in a circular fashion around each plate. Place the vegetable mixture in the middle of the pork. Drizzle the sauce over all and serve immediately.

YIELD: 4 SERVINGS

Chocolate Bourbon Pecan Tart

Crust:
2 cups all-purpose flour
1/8 teaspoon salt
1/2 teaspoon granulated sugar
1/4 cup (1/2 stick) cold butter, cubed
2 tablespoons vegetable shortening
8 to 10 tablespoons water

Filling:
3 eggs
3/4 cup packed light brown sugar
2/3 cup dark corn syrup
1/2 cup (1 stick) butter
1/8 teaspoon salt
4 tablespoons bourbon whiskey
1 teaspoon pure vanilla extract
2 cups chocolate chips
2 cups pecan halves

To make the crust: In a medium-sized bowl, sift together the flour, salt, and sugar. Cut in the butter and shortening with fingertips until the dough looks like coarse meal. Sprinkle with the water and blend until combined. Form into a ball and wrap with plastic wrap. Chill for 30 minutes.

Roll out the chilled dough on a floured surface and fit snugly in a 9-inch tart pan. Set aside.

Preheat oven to 375° F. To make the filling: In a medium-sized bowl, mix together the eggs, sugar, syrup, butter, salt, whiskey, and vanilla.

Sprinkle the chocolate chips on top of the reserved crust and layer the pecans on top of the chocolate chips. Pour the filling over the pecans and bake for 40 minutes. Let cool for 10 minutes on a wire rack. Serve.

YIELD: 6 TO 8 SERVINGS

Sautéed Shrimp with Endive, Leeks & Pernod Sauce

1 recipe *Pernod Sauce* (see recipe
  below)
1 tablespoon Cajun seafood spice
1/8 teaspoon salt
1/8 teaspoon freshly ground black
  pepper
2 tablespoons butter
12 fresh jumbo shrimp (10 to 15
  count), peeled and deveined with
  tails
2 tablespoons dry vermouth
2 heads endive, rinsed, dried, and
  julienned; reserve 12 leaves
1 bunch leeks, well cleaned and
  julienned (white part only)
Salt and freshly ground black pepper
  to taste
1/4 cup heavy cream
2 medium fresh tomatoes, finely
  diced

In a stainless steel bowl, mix together
the seafood spice and the 1/8 teaspoons
salt and black pepper. Toss the shrimp in
the spices. In a large skillet, melt the
butter and sauté the shrimp for 2 to 3
minutes. Keep warm.

Deglaze the skillet with the vermouth. Stir in the endive, leeks, salt, and
black pepper and sauté for 3 to 5 minutes
or until tender. Add the cream and
reduce to sauce consistency. Keep warm.

Ladle 1/4 cup *Pernod Sauce* in the
center of each plate. Arrange 3 shrimp
(tail out) touching in the center of the
plate. Place 3 endive leaves in between
each shrimp and place 1 to 2 tablespoons
of the leek mixture at the base of each
endive. Sprinkle the diced tomato over
the shrimp and serve immediately.

YIELD: 4 SERVINGS

Pernod Sauce

1 tablespoon butter
1 tablespoon finely chopped garlic
1/4 cup Pernod liqueur
2 cups heavy cream

In a medium-sized saucepan, melt the
butter and sauté the garlic for 3 to 5
minutes or until tender. Add the liqueur
and 1 cup of the cream and reduce by
half. Stir in the remaining cream and
reduce to sauce consistency.

Roasted Lamb Loin with Black Bean, Corn & Mango Salsa

1 recipe *Black Bean, Corn & Mango Salsa* (see recipe below)
4 racks of lamb
$^1/_4$ cup hazelnut oil
6 tablespoons jerk seasoning
$^1/_8$ teaspoon salt
$^1/_8$ teaspoon freshly ground black pepper
Fresh mint, chopped
Fresh cilantro, chopped

Pastry:
3 cups canola oil
2 phyllo pastry sheets

Sauce:
4 tablespoons olive oil
2 sprigs fresh rosemary
3 sprigs fresh mint
Salt and freshly ground black pepper to taste
3 tablespoons sweet vermouth
$^1/_4$ cup honey
4 cups vegetable stock

Preheat oven to 350° F. Clean the lamb loin from the racks and reserve the bones. In a stainless steel bowl, mix together the hazelnut oil, jerk seasoning, salt, and black pepper. Evenly coat each loin in the mixture. In a large, hot skillet, sear each side of the loins. Place the loins in a baking pan and bake for 15 to 20 minutes. Keep warm.

To make the pastry: In a shallow saucepan, heat the oil to 350° F. Cut the pastry sheets in half, then into 4 triangles. Place each triangle, one at a time, in the oil and lightly brown on both sides. Remove from oil, shape into half circles long side, and drain on paper towels.

To make the sauce: In a large saucepan, heat the oil and sauté the reserved lamb bones, rosemary, mint, salt, and black pepper until the bones are browned. Deglaze the saucepan with the vermouth. Stir in the honey and stock and reduce by half. Strain and keep warm.

Slice each loin into 5 to 7 even slices. Ladle $^1/_4$ cup of the sauce onto each plate. Place 1 pastry triangle in the center and spoon $^1/_2$ cup *Black Bean, Corn & Mango Salsa* on the triangle. Shingle the lamb slices down and around the salsa. Sprinkle with the mint and cilantro and serve immediately.

YIELD: 4 SERVINGS

Black Bean, Corn & Mango Salsa

2 cups cooked black beans
1 cup finely diced fresh mango
1 cup steamed fresh corn
$^1/_2$ tablespoon finely chopped fresh cilantro
Freshly ground black pepper to taste
1 clove garlic, finely chopped
2 tablespoons fresh orange juice
1 tablespoon fresh lime juice
Salt to taste

In a stainless steel bowl, mix together all of the ingredients, except the salt, and chill for 1 hour. Add the salt shortly before serving.

Roasted Anjou Pears with Blackberry Sauce & Stilton Blue Cheese Quenelles

1 recipe *Stilton Blue Cheese Quenelles* (see recipe below)
1 recipe *Blackberry Sauce* (see recipe below)
3 tablespoons butter
4 medium Anjou pears, peeled, cored, and quartered lengthwise
48 whole blackberries, rinsed

Preheat oven to 450° F. In a large baking dish, melt the butter and brown the pears on medium heat for 10 minutes, turning often to color evenly. Place in oven and bake for 7 minutes or until tender.

Ladle the *Blackberry Sauce* into 4 half-dollar sized pools on each plate. Place 1 quarter piece of pear on top of each pool of sauce and arrange a cluster of 3 black-berries between each piece of pear. Place 3 *Stilton Blue Cheese Quenelles* in the center of each plate and serve immediately.

YIELD: 4 SERVINGS

Stilton Blue Cheese Quenelles

4 ounces Stilton blue cheese
1 tablespoon honey
1 tablepoon heavy cream

In a food processor, puree the cheese, honey, and cream for 40 seconds, or until the mixture is smoothly blended. Chill for 30 minutes.

With 2 demitasse spoons, make 12 quenelles: Place 1 spoon in a bowl of cold water. With the other spoon, scoop out enough of the chilled mixture to just fill the spoon. Invert the moist other spoon over the filled spoon and shape into egg-shaped pieces. Place on a wax paper-covered baking sheet and repeat the procedure for 11 more quenelles. Chill.

Blackberry Sauce

3 cups rinsed fresh blackberries
1 tablespoon confectioners' sugar
Juice of 1 lemon

In a food processor, puree the black-berries, sugar, and lemon juice for 30 seconds. Strain into a bowl through a fine-mesh strainer and set aside.

Jalapeño & Roasted Corn Soup

10 ears fresh corn, shucked
3 tablespoons olive oil
3 tablespoons butter
1 cup chopped Vidalia onions
4 jalapeño chili peppers
1 teaspoon finely chopped garlic
2 teaspoons chopped fresh basil
Salt and freshly ground black pepper to taste
4 tablespoons all-purpose flour
$1/4$ cup granulated sugar
4 cups chicken stock
$1/2$ cup heavy cream
$1/2$ cup chopped fresh chives
8 fresh chive stems
$1/2$ cup sour cream

Preheat oven to 375° F. Cover a baking sheet with parchment paper. Rub the corn with the oil. Place on the prepared baking sheet and roast for 45 minutes, turning twice for even browning.

In a large pot, melt the butter and sauté the onions, chili peppers, garlic, basil, salt, and black pepper for 3 to 5 minutes, or until the onions and chili peppers are tender. Dust the mixture with the flour and sugar, stirring until absorbed. Cut the kernels from the corn cobs and set aside. Add the cobs and stock to the pot and and bring to a boil. Reduce heat to simmer and remove the cobs.

In a blender or food processor, puree the soup with two-thirds of the reserved corn kernels until smooth. Return the soup to the pot and whisk in the cream. Stir half of the remaining corn kernels into the soup. In a small bowl, mix together the other half of the corn kernels and the chopped chives.

Ladle the soup into bowls and garnish each bowl with a dollop of the sour cream, topped with 1 tablespoon of the corn/chive mixture. Lay 2 whole chives across the top and serve immediately.

YIELD: 4 SERVINGS

Tuna Loin Wrapped in Pancétta with Gazpacho, Roasted Parmesan & Sun-Dried Tomato Polenta

1 recipe *Sun-Dried Tomato Polenta*
  (see recipe below)
1 recipe *Gazpacho* (see recipe below)
1 recipe *Butter Sauce* (see recipe
  below)
2 tablespoons Dijon mustard
Four 3-ounce center-cut fresh tuna
  loins, trimmed
1 teaspoon salt
1 teaspoon freshly ground black
  pepper
4 slices pancétta
2 tablespoons butter
Fresh cilantro, chopped

Once again one of our "Inn Country Chefs" has introduced an innovative, wonderfully simple, summer dinner party idea that will surprise and delight you and your guests. The rich flavor of the pancétta enhances the fresh tuna and blossoms to full flower when the gazpacho with roasted Parmesan is added. The standard seafood rule applies: Always make certain of the absolute freshness of your tuna.

Roasted Parmesan:
1 $^1/_2$ cups freshly grated Parmesan cheese

Preheat oven to 350° F. Spread the mustard on the loins and season with the salt and black pepper. Wrap each loin with 1 slice of the pancétta and hold in place with a toothpick. In a large sauté pan, melt the butter and sear the loins on all sides. Place in a baking pan and bake for 10 to 12 minutes or until medium rare. Keep warm.

Preheat oven to 250° F. To make the roasted Parmesan: Cover a baking sheet with parchment paper. Sprinkle the cheese on the prepared baking sheet and bake for 10 to 12 minutes, or until the cheese is melted and crispy. Let cool. Gently break into 12 pieces and set aside.

Remove the chilled polenta from the metal rings. In a large sauté pan, melt the remaining 2 tablespoons butter and brown each circle of polenta on both sides. Return the polenta to the lined baking sheet and keep warm.

Ladle ³/₄ cup *Gazpacho* into each large, shallow plate. Place 1 circle of the *Sun-Dried Tomato Polenta* in the center of each plate. Remove the toothpick from each loin and place the loin on top of the polenta. Drizzle ¹/₄ cup *Butter Sauce* over each loin and surroundings.

Garnish each plate with 3 pieces of the roasted Parmesan by arranging each piece around the loin, creating a pyramid effect. Sprinkle with the cilantro and serve immediately.

YIELD: 4 SERVINGS

Sun-Dried Tomato Polenta

³/₄ cup water

³/₄ cup cornmeal

¹/₂ cup chicken stock

¹/₄ cup freshly grated Parmesan cheese

1 tablepoon sun-dried tomatoes in oil

2 tablespoons heavy cream

2 tablespoons butter

Salt and freshly ground black pepper
   to taste

Cover a baking sheet with parchment paper and place four 3-inch metal rings on the paper. In a stainless steel bowl, mix together the water and cornmeal and set aside.

In a medium-sized saucepan, bring the stock to a full boil and gradually stir in the reserved cornmeal mixture until well blended. Reduce heat to simmer and cook until thick, stirring frequently.

Remove from heat and stir in the cheese, tomatoes, cream, butter, salt, and black pepper. Pour the mixture in the metal rings on the prepared baking sheet and chill until firm.

Gazpacho

¹/₄ cup finely diced zucchini

¹/₄ cup finely diced yellow summer squash

¹/₄ cup finely diced celery

¹/₄ cup finely diced yellow bell peppers

¹/₄ cup finely diced red bell peppers

¹/₄ cup finely diced fresh Italian plum tomatoes

$^{1}/_{2}$ tablespoon finely chopped garlic
$^{1}/_{2}$ tablespoon chopped fresh cilantro
$^{3}/_{4}$ teaspoon Tabasco sauce
1 tablespoon julienned fresh basil
1 teaspoon salt
1 teaspoon freshly ground white pepper
$^{3}/_{4}$ cup pureed stewed tomatoes
$^{3}/_{4}$ cup V-8 juice

In a stainless steel bowl, mix together all of the fresh vegetables, the garlic, cilantro, Tabasco sauce, basil, salt, and white pepper. In a small bowl, combine the stewed tomatoes and the V-8 juice. Pour the tomato mixture over the vegetable mixture and stir to blend well. Chill for 1 hour.

Butter Sauce

6 tablespoons ($^{3}/_{4}$ stick) butter
6 shallots, chopped
1 clove garlic, finely chopped
$^{1}/_{4}$ cup golden sherry
2 cups heavy cream
$^{1}/_{4}$ cup ($^{1}/_{2}$ stick) cold butter, cubed

In a large saucepan, melt the 6 tablespoons butter and sauté the shallots and garlic for 4 to 6 minutes or until golden brown. Deglaze the saucepan with the sherry. Add the cream and reduce to a sauce consistency. Remove from heat and whisk in the cold butter. Strain and keep warm.

Chapter 12

Spinach Salad with Piñons & Raspberry Vinaigrette

Speared Italian Tomato Rounds with Sweet Basil Pesto

Chocolate Waffles with Lemon Spanish Cream Custard

Tomato Bisque & Black Olive Paste on Yellow Corn Triangles

Spicy Marinated Vegetable Salad

Lamb & Pork Phyllo Twists with Orzo
& Shiitake Mushroom Sauce

Green Chili-Corn Soup

Grilled Salmon Steaks & Black Bean Paste
with Red Chili Sauce & Mango Salsa

CHEF PAT WALTER
Grant Corner Inn, Santa Fe, New Mexico

COURTESY PAT WALTER

PAT WALTER
Grant Corner Inn, Santa Fe, New Mexico

For the past few decades, Santa Fe has been busy developing a style all its own. It was a genuine love of all things New Mexican that drove Pat Walter to nurture his interest in environmental design and his avocation as a sculptor. Like a lot of the most innovative people I have met in the business of keeping an inn, Pat found a way to satisfy his creative bent in the kitchen. With his wife Louise and daughter Bumpy handling other inn management details, Pat has succeeded in combining persistence, creativity, and curiosity into a sensational lifestyle "salsa" that is known as Grant Corner Inn.

One of my personal favorite Pat Walter kitchen tricks showed up on a brunch plate the first time I visited Pat in his inn kitchen. On this particular day, Pat carefully sliced a jícama into $1/8$-inch thick slices and using a stylish cookie cutter shaped like a saguaro cactus, he carefully cut out several jícama "cacti" and placed them into a green mint solution to soak for several minutes. Pat then placed them carefully into the refried beans and thus, a lowly root vegetable had been transformed into the "star" of a beautifully composed New Mexican brunch platter, which could only come from Santa Fe and the creative mind of Pat Walter.

Without a doubt, the one constant that intrepid inngoers quickly discover is the singularly unique atmosphere at every inn along the way. Combine that with the Santa Fe-style and the talent of a designer turned chef like Pat Walter, and you end up with some of the most unusual and exciting recipes in the entire "Inn Country Chefs" series.

Spinach Salad with Piñons & Raspberry Vinaigrette

2 bunches fresh spinach, rinsed, trimmed, and dried
1 cup roasted piñon nuts
1 pint fresh raspberries, rinsed
1 clove garlic, finely chopped
$^1/_4$ cup white wine vinegar
$^1/_2$ cup extra-virgin olive oil
1 tablespoon brown sugar or to taste

Arrange the spinach on each salad plate petal style, with the largest leaves circling outside of the plate and the smaller leaves spiraling to the center of the plate. Chill the salads.

In a food processor, finely chop the nuts (do not puree) and set aside.

In a blender, puree the raspberries. Strain to remove seeds. Return the berry puree to the blender, add the remaining ingredients, and blend until well combined.

Drizzle the raspberry vinaigrette over the chilled spinach leaves and lightly sprinkle the reserved nuts over the entire salad and plate edge. Serve immediately.

YIELD: 6 SERVINGS

Speared Italian Tomato Rounds with Sweet Basil Pesto

1 cup fresh basil leaves
$^1/_2$ cup olive oil
1 tablespoon piñon nuts
1 clove garlic, chopped
$^1/_2$ teaspoon salt
8 small firm fresh Italian plum tomatoes
2 bunches fresh baby asparagus
$^1/_2$ cup freshly grated Parmesan cheese

In a blender or food processor, blend together the basil, oil, nuts, garlic, and salt. Cut the tomatoes into thick, even slices. Punch a hole in the lower half of each tomato slice and insert asparagus spears.

Arrange the tomato rounds in a crescent shape on each plate and drizzle the pesto over the salad. Sprinkle the cheese over the lower half of the salad and plate and serve immediately.

YIELD: 8 APPETIZER SERVINGS

Chocolate Waffles
with Lemon Spanish Cream Custard

1 recipe *Lemon Spanish Cream
  Custard* (see recipe below)
6 eggs, separated
6 tablespoons granulated sugar
²/₃ cup all-purpose flour
¹/₂ cup Spanish cocoa mix

2 teaspoons baking powder
Pinch salt
¹/₂ cup milk
¹/₄ cup vegetable oil
Zest of 1 orange

Preheat a waffle iron. In a medium-sized bowl, beat the egg yolks and sugar until smooth and light. In a small bowl, sift together the flour, cocoa mix, baking powder, and salt. Stir the flour mixture into the egg yolk mixture. Add the milk and oil and beat together to form a smooth batter.

Pour the batter into the waffle iron and bake until golden. Repeat until all of the batter is used.

Divide the waffles among the plates and arrange in a double fan. Ladle ¹/₄ cup *Lemon Spanish Cream Custard* over the waffles and garnish with the zest. Serve immediately.
YIELD: 8 SERVINGS

Lemon Spanish Cream Custard

4 egg yolks, beaten
Pinch salt
¹/₄ cup granulated sugar
2 cups scalded cooled milk
2 teaspoons lemon zest
1 teaspoon pure vanilla extract

In a large double boiler over simmering water, mix together the egg yolks, salt, and sugar. Gradually stir in the milk and cook on low heat, stirring constantly, until the mixture coats a metal spoon. Gently stir in the zest and vanilla. Chill.

Tomato Bisque & Black Olive Paste on Yellow Corn Triangles

$^1/_4$ cup ($^1/_2$ stick) butter

2 small white onions, finely chopped

2 cloves garlic, finely chopped

2 medium carrots, finely chopped

10 medium fresh tomatoes, peeled and cut into wedges

2 tablespoons chopped fresh basil

2 tablespoons chopped fresh thyme

2 tablespoons chopped fresh oregano

Salt and freshly ground black pepper to taste

1 recipe *Black Olive Paste* (see recipe below)

1 $^1/_2$ cups half-and-half

Lemon slices

Fresh parsley, finely chopped

Yellow corn chips

> Whenever I come across unique and tantalizing appetizers on a menu anywhere, I will generally end up making a meal of several of them and never get to the entrée. Chef Walter's *Tomato Bisque & Black Olive Paste on Yellow Corn Triangles* is just that type of appetizer. This undeniably southwestern taste sensation works equally well as a starter, or for a different twist, serve on a buffet with chips and dips!

In a large sauté pan, melt the butter and sauté the onions and garlic for 3 to 5 minutes, or until the onions are translucent. Add the carrots and tomatoes and simmer for 30 minutes.

Stir in the herbs, salt, and black pepper and continue to simmer for 10 minutes more. Add the half-and-half and stir just until hot.

Ladle the bisque into soup plates. Garnish with the lemon slices and sprinkle with the parsley. Spread the *Black Olive Paste* on the corn chips and arrange around the plate. Serve immediately.

YIELD: 6 SERVINGS

Black Olive Paste

One 15-ounce can gourmet pitted black olives, drained
2 tablespoons extra-virgin olive oil
1 medium clove garlic, coarsely chopped
1 green onion, chopped
Pinch salt or to taste

In a food processor, combine all of the ingredients and process until reach a coarse paste.

Spicy Marinated Vegetable Salad

1 clove garlic, finely chopped
1 tablespoon granulated sugar
$^3/_4$ cup red wine vinegar
$^3/_4$ cup olive oil
$^1/_4$ cup hot sesame oil
1 teaspoon salt or to taste
$^1/_4$ teaspoon freshly ground white
  pepper or to taste
3 medium zucchini, thinly sliced
3 medium yellow summer squash,
  thinly sliced

4 medium carrots, medium diced
1 medium jícama, medium diced
1 medium red bell pepper, seeded,
  deveined, and medium diced
$^1/_4$ medium red onion, finely chopped
3 tablespoons chopped fresh cilantro
2 Granny Smith apples, peeled and
  medium diced
1 head butter lettuce, rinsed, dried,
  and leaves separated

In a large bowl, whisk together the garlic, sugar, vinegar, both oils, salt, and white pepper. Add the zucchini, squash, carrots, jícama, bell pepper, onion, and cilantro and toss together until well coated with the marinade.

Cover the bowl with plastic wrap and chill overnight. Add the apples and toss to combine.

Place several lettuce leaves on each plate and spoon the salad on top. Serve immediately.

YIELD: 6 SERVINGS

Lamb & Pork Phyllo Twists with Orzo & Shiitake Mushroom Sauce

1 pound ground pork
1 pound ground lamb
1 tablespoon chopped fresh basil
2 teaspoons finely chopped garlic
1 teaspoon salt
$1/2$ teaspoon freshly ground black pepper
2 tablespoons olive oil
4 quarts water
1 teaspoon salt
2 cups uncooked orzo pasta
20 phyllo pastry sheets, thawed
1 $1/2$ sticks butter, melted
1 recipe *Shiitake Mushroom Sauce* (see recipe below)
Fresh tarragon, coarsely chopped

Preheat oven to 350° F. In a medium-sized bowl, mix together the pork, lamb, basil, garlic, salt, and black pepper and make into 1 $1/2$-inch meatballs. In a baking dish, add the oil, then the meatballs and bake for about 40 minutes.

Meanwhile, in a large pot, bring the water to a rapid boil. Add the salt, then add the orzo, stirring occasionally, until desired tenderness. Drain and keep warm.

Cut the pastry in half sheets (5 x 6 inches). Brush both sides of the sheets with the butter. Place 3 sheets together (divided with wax paper) and cover all of the pastry with damp cloths to keep moist.

Preheat oven to 350° F. Remove the wax paper and wrap each meatball in 3 sheets of pastry, twisting like a package with flared ends. Place the twists on a baking sheet and bake for 25 minutes or until browned.

Scoop the orzo onto each plate and place 2 twists on top of the orzo. Ladle $1/4$ to $1/2$ cup *Shiitake Mushroom Sauce* on the rim of the plate and garnish with the tarragon. Serve immediately. Serve remaining sauce on the side.

YIELD: 6 SERVINGS

Shiitake Mushroom Sauce

1 stick butter, melted
4 tablespoons chopped white onions
8 ounces fresh shiitake mushrooms, chopped
2 cups beef stock
1 teaspoon liquid smoke
3 cloves garlic, finely chopped
3 smoked or dried chipotle or habanero chili peppers, chopped
Salt and freshly ground black pepper to taste

In a small skillet, melt the butter and sauté the onions for 3 to 5 minutes or until translucent. Add the mushrooms and lightly sauté on medium heat until tender.

In a blender or food processor, combine the mushroom mixture and the remaining ingredients and blend together until coarsely pureed. In a medium-sized saucepan, simmer the mixture for 15 minutes on medium heat. Serve hot. Makes about 4 cups.

Green Chili-Corn Soup

5 tablespoons vegetable oil
4 medium white onions, finely chopped
2 cloves garlic, finely chopped
1 medium red bell pepper, seeded, deveined, and chopped
4 cups cooked corn kernels
1 cup cooked green chili peppers
2 medium russet potatoes, peeled and boiled
5 cups chicken stock
$^1/_2$ cup half-and-half
1 teaspoon salt
$^1/_4$ teaspoon freshly ground white pepper

In a large saucepan, heat the oil and sauté the onions and garlic for 3 to 5 minutes, or until the onions are translucent. Add the bell pepper and sauté for 4 minutes. Add the corn and sauté for 5 minutes more. Mix in the chili peppers and stock and simmer for 30 minutes, stirring occasionally.

In a blender or food processor, blend the mixture in small batches and return to the saucepan. Stir in the half-and-half, salt, and white pepper and simmer for 10 minutes.

Ladle the soup into bowls and serve immediately.

Yield: 6 servings

Grilled Salmon Steaks & Black Bean Paste with Red Chili Sauce & Mango Salsa

1 recipe *Black Bean Paste* (see recipe below)
1 recipe *Red Chili Sauce* (see recipe below)
1 recipe *Mango Salsa* (see recipe below)
Six 10-ounce fresh salmon steaks
Fresh lemon juice
Melted butter

Place the steaks on a hot, oiled broiler pan, brushing often with the lemon juice and butter, and grill for 3 to 4 minutes on each side, or until the salmon flakes.

Cover each plate with the *Black Bean Paste* and place 1 steak on top of the paste. Top with the *Mango Salsa* and drizzle the *Red Chili Sauce* over all. Serve immediately.

YIELD: 6 SERVINGS

Black Bean Paste

Two 16-ounce bags dried black beans
2 tablespoons butter
1 bunch green onions, chopped
1 teaspoon finely chopped garlic
2 tablespoons dark molasses
4 tablespoons bacon fat
$^{1}/_{2}$ teaspoon salt

In a large pot, soak the beans overnight with enough water to cover 3 inches. Bring to a boil. Reduce heat to simmer and cook for 1 hour 30 minutes or until tender. Drain and mash.

In a small skillet, melt the butter and sauté the onions and garlic for 3 to 5 minutes or until tender. In a large saucepan, combine the onion mixture, molasses, bacon fat, and salt and heat through. Add the mashed beans and mix together well. Heat on low heat, stirring frequently, for 10 minutes, or until the liquid reduces and the beans thicken.

Red Chili Sauce

3/4 cup beef stock
1/4 cup red chili powder
1/2 cup melted bacon fat
1 teaspoon salt
1/2 teaspoon freshly ground white
  pepper

2 cloves garlic, chopped and pureed
1/2 large white onion, chopped and
  pureed
1 tablespoon finely chopped fresh
  cilantro

In a small saucepan, mix together all of the ingredients and cook on medium-high heat, stirring constantly, until slightly thick. If needed, add hot water to thin.

Pour the sauce into a squeeze bottle for drizzling.

Mango Salsa

2 tablespoons butter
4 green onions, chopped
1/2 medium red onion, chopped
1 clove garlic, finely chopped
1/2 medium red bell pepper, chopped
1/2 medium green bell pepper,
  chopped

2 ripe mangos, chopped
1/3 cup chopped fresh cilantro
2 tablespoons balsamic vinegar
Juice of 1 lime

In a medium-sized skillet, melt the butter and sauté all of the onions and the garlic for 3 to 5 minutes or until tender-crisp. Let cool.

In a small bowl, combine the cooled onion mixture and the remaining ingredients and mix together well.

As far as I know, there are not many salmon running the rivers and streams in and around Santa Fe, but here is another example of a product that is not indigenous to a specific area, but being adapted and improved with local ingredients and flavors. Once you try this combination, you will find it difficult to go back to the standard lemon-dill accompaniment to your fresh salmon. This recipe works very well with all firm-flesh fish, so be adventurous!

Chapter 13

Tomato Consommé

Pacific Salmon with Rosemary–Mustard Sauce

Crème Brûlée Trio

Chocolate Cake

Spaghetti Squash Cake

Summer Squash Timbale with Wild Mushroom Risotto

Bread Pudding with B & B

Sea Scallops with Honey & Curry

Dungeness Crab-Stuffed Prawns with Vanilla Butter Cream Sauce

Wild Berry Cobbler with Lemon Curd Sauce

CHEF JEAN-LOUIS HAMICHE
Carter House/Hotel Carter, Eureka, California

COURTESY CARTER HOUSE/HOTEL CARTER

CHEF JEAN-LOUIS HAMICHE
Carter House/Hotel Carter,
Eureka, California

Jean-Louis is living proof that the best chefs in the world are probably taught by their grandmothers! According to Mark Carter, owner and innkeeper of the famous Carter House and the popular Hotel Carter across the street, the highest praise a chef can receive is to have his dishes described as "unforgettable" by satisfied guests, and Jean-Louis hears that compliment everyday. Born in Marseilles, France, Chef Hamiche shares his love for the celebration of food and wine with the Carters, whose California lifestyle has taught them deep appreciation for the same things. Meals at the Hotel Carter are more of an event than simply a time to eat, since Jean-Louis arrived in Eureka.

For Chef Hamiche, success in the kitchen begins in the garden. In the incredible kitchen garden that Mark and Jean-Louis designed and manage with the help of several full-time gardeners, you will find more hybrid varieties of basil and mint than you ever knew existed. Selected, perfectly grown green beans, bell peppers, and unique edible flowers abound. In fact, the Carters often host Country French-styled peasant dinners of roast chicken, oysters on the half shell, and roasted corn on the cob on a long wooden table placed in the center of their beautiful garden. Nature's own dining room!

Tomato Consommé

6 cups diced fresh tomatoes, peeled and seeded
6 cups tomato juice
1 bunch fresh basil, finely chopped
3 cups chicken stock
1 medium onion, diced
2 cups diced celery
1 cup blanched fresh fava beans

In a large saucepan, combine all of the ingredients, except the beans, and cook on medium heat, stirring frequently, for 1 hour. Strain 3 times through cheesecloth.

Ladle the consommé into bowls and garnish with the beans. Serve immediately.

YIELD: 4 TO 6 SERVINGS

Pacific Salmon with Rosemary-Mustard Sauce

1 recipe *Rosemary-Mustard Sauce* (see recipe below)
Four 8-ounce fresh salmon fillets
Salt and freshly ground black pepper to taste
1 tablespoon olive oil
1 tablespoon butter, melted
4 sprigs fresh rosemary, rinsed

Season the fillets with the salt and black pepper. In a large skillet, heat the oil and butter and sauté the fillets on both sides until golden.

Ladle ¼ cup *Rosemary-Mustard Sauce* on each plate and place 1 fillet on top of the sauce. Garnish each serving with 1 rosemary sprig and serve immediately.

YIELD: 4 SERVINGS

Rosemary-Mustard Sauce

1 tablespoon butter
2 shallots, finely chopped
1 cup dry white wine
3 sprigs fresh rosemary, rinsed
1 cup cream
1 ½ tablespoons Dijon mustard

> With the waters of the North Pacific literally walking distance from their garden, it is not surprising to find fresh salmon and rosemary meeting on a plate in the Carters' dining room. The rosemary-mustard sauce used in this recipe works beautifully with many baked and roasted meats, but this combination is an unusually elegant taste sensation.

In a medium-sized saucepan, melt the butter and sauté the shallots for 4 to 5 minutes. Add the wine and rosemary and reduce by half. Mix in the cream and cook until slightly thick. Stir in the mustard and heat through.

Crème Brûlée Trio

3 cups cream
One 2-inch strip vanilla bean
8 egg yolks
$^1/_2$ cup granulated sugar
1 $^1/_2$ cups fresh raspberries
Granulated sugar to taste
1 $^1/_2$ cups semisweet chocolate chips
$^1/_2$ cup cream

In a large saucepan, scald the 3 cups cream with the vanilla bean. In a medium-sized bowl, whisk together the eggs and the $^1/_2$ cup sugar. Add the egg mixture to the cream mixture and stir until well combined.

In a blender or food processor, combine the raspberries and sugar to taste and puree until well blended. In the top of a double boiler over simmering water, melt the chocolate chips. Add the $^1/_2$ cup cream and stir until smooth and heated through.

Divide the combined egg and cream mixture into three bowls. Flavor one-third with the raspberry puree, flavor one-third with the chocolate mixture, and the remaining third remains unflavored.

Preheat oven to 350° F. Pour the raspberry-flavored mixture into 4 ramekins, the chocolate-flavored mixture into 4 ramekins, and the unflavored mixture into 4 ramekins. Place the ramekins in 1 large baking pan and fill two-thirds up the sides of the dishes with hot water. Bake for 45 minutes or until firm.

Place 3 ramekins (1 each of the three flavors) on each plate and serve immediately.
YIELD: 4 SERVINGS

Chocolate Cake

1 pound semisweet chocolate
2 tablespoons unsalted butter
4 eggs, separated
1 tablespoon all-purpose flour
1 tablespoon granulated sugar
$^1/_2$ teaspoon salt
Vanilla ice cream

In the top of a large double boiler over simmering water, melt the chocolate, then stir in the butter. In a small bowl, beat the egg yolks, then mix in the flour. Fold the egg yolk mixture into the chocolate mixture.

Preheat oven to 400° F. In a medium-sized bowl, beat the egg whites until soft peaks form. Add the sugar and salt and fold the egg white mixture, one-third at a time, into the chocolate mixture.

Gently pour the mixture into a buttered 9-inch springform pan and bake for 18 minutes. Let cool. Chill overnight. Serve with the ice cream.

YIELD: 6 SERVINGS

Spaghetti Squash Cake

1 spaghetti squash, halved and seeded
1 medium onion, chopped
4 cloves garlic, finely chopped
1 medium red bell pepper, seeded, deveined, and chopped
1 medium zucchini, grated
4 eggs, beaten
$1/2$ cup all-purpose flour
1 teaspoon ground paprika
2 teaspoons chili powder
Salt and freshly ground black pepper to taste
4 tablespoons extra-virgin olive oil
2 teaspoons balsamic vinegar
Pinch salt
Fresh mixed baby greens, rinsed and dried

Preheat oven to 350° F. Place the squash in a baking pan and bake for 35 to 45 minutes or until tender. Let cool.

Scoop out the squash meat and place in a large bowl. Add the onion, garlic, bell pepper, zucchini, eggs, and flour and mix together well. Stir in the paprika, chili powder, salt, and black pepper.

In a large, hot skillet, heat 2 tablespoons of the oil and fry the squash mixture like small pancakes for 3 minutes on each side or until golden. Remove and keep warm until all of the squash mixture is fried.

In a small bowl, whisk together the remaining oil, the vinegar, and salt. Lightly toss the greens with the dressing.

Divide the dressed greens among small plates and place 3 small squash cakes on top of the greens. Serve immediately.

YIELD: 6 APPETIZER SERVINGS

Summer Squash Timbale with Wild Mushroom Risotto

4 cups grated baby summer squash
Salt
2 tablespoons extra-virgin olive oil
1 medium yellow onion, finely chopped
1 teaspoon finely chopped garlic
3 tablespoons finely chopped mixed fresh herbs (any type)
5 eggs, beaten
2 cups heavy cream
Salt and freshly ground black pepper to taste
Butter
1 cup dried French bread crumbs
1 recipe *Wild Mushroom Risotto* (see recipe below)
1 cup freshly grated Parmesan cheese
Fresh herb sprigs

Place the squash in a colander set over a bowl and generously sprinkle with the salt. Mix with fingertips to distribute salt evenly. Let stand for 30 minutes.

In a small skillet, heat the oil and sauté the onion and garlic for 3 to 5 minutes, or until the onion is translucent. Set aside.

Gather the squash in both hands and gently squeeze to release any additional surface moisture. In a large bowl, combine the squash, reserved onion mixture, and the 3 tablespoons mixed herbs. Mix in the eggs, cream, salt, and black pepper.

Preheat oven to 350° F. Butter the bottom and sides of a 5-cup mold and dust with the bread crumbs to coat completely. Shake out any excess crumbs.

Fill the prepared mold with the squash mixture and place the mold in a baking pan with enough hot water to reach two-thirds up the sides of the mold. Bake, uncovered, for 1 hour or until set.

Remove from oven and let stand for 5 minutes. Run a thin-bladed knife around the inside edge of the mold and invert onto a serving platter. Sprinkle with the cheese and garnish with the herb sprigs. Serve immediately with the *Wild Mushroom Risotto*.

YIELD: 4 TO 6 SERVINGS

Wild Mushroom Risotto

1 tablespoon unsalted butter
3 tablespoons olive oil
$^1/_2$ medium onion, chopped
8 cloves garlic, finely chopped
1 cup uncooked arborio rice
$^1/_2$ cup dry white wine
4 cups vegetable or chicken stock
1 pound fresh chanterelle mushrooms, trimmed and sliced
Juice of 1 lemon
$^1/_4$ cup chopped fresh parsley
Dash ground nutmeg
Salt and freshly ground black pepper to taste
$^1/_2$ cup freshly grated Parmesan cheese

In a large saucepan, heat the butter and 1 tablespoon of the oil and sauté the onion and 4 cloves of the garlic for 3 to 5 minutes, or until the onion is translucent. Add the rice and sauté for 1 minute. Add the wine and cook until reduced by half.

Stir in the stock, $^1/_4$ cup at a time, and simmer until the liquid is absorbed, stirring frequently, and adding more stock until the rice is cooked, about 15 to 20 minutes.

Meanwhile, in a large skillet, heat the remaining oil and sauté the mushrooms and remaining garlic with the lemon juice, parsley, nutmeg, salt, and black pepper until the mushrooms are tender. Stir the mushroom mixture into the rice mixture. Add the cheese and mix together well. Serve hot.

Bread Pudding with B & B

1 loaf stale French bread, cut into $1/2$-inch slices
4 eggs, beaten
1 $1/2$ cups granulated sugar
6 cups milk
2 cups heavy cream
1 cup melted unsalted butter
4 teaspoons pure vanilla extract
2 teaspoons pure almond extract
1 cup raisins
1 cup dried apricots
Freshly grated nutmeg
2 tablespoons B & B liqueur or more

In a large bowl, place the bread slices. In another bowl, mix together the next ten ingredients and pour over the bread slices. Let stand for 30 minutes.

Preheat oven to 350° F. Pour the mixture into a buttered 2 $1/2$- to 3-quart baking dish and bake for 1 hour or until set.

Remove from oven and let cool slightly. Drizzle the liqueur over the top and serve immediately.

YIELD: 4 TO 6 SERVINGS

Leave it to Jean-Louis to take a traditional, sometimes unexciting bread pudding and turn it into the kind of dessert that you will want to eat first. When you drizzle the Bénédictine & Brandy over the bread pudding, I can assure you every glass in the room will be raised in a toast to your creativity and mastery of this exciting dessert. A delightful finish!

Sea Scallops with Honey & Curry

1 cup honey
$1/_4$ cup curry powder
12 fresh sea scallops

In a large saucepan, stir together the honey and curry powder and bring to a boil. Reduce heat to medium and cook, stirring constantly, until syrupy. Add the scallops and cook for 2 to 4 minutes, depending on the size of the scallops.

Place 3 scallops on each small plate and cover with the sauce. Serve immediately.

YIELD: 4 APPETIZER SERVINGS

Dungeness Crab-Stuffed Prawns with Vanilla Butter Cream Sauce

1 recipe *Vanilla Butter Cream Sauce* (see recipe below)
16 large fresh prawns (10 to 15 count), peeled, deveined, and butterflied
Melted butter
4 sprigs fresh fennel

Stuffing:
1 cup shredded fresh Dungeness crabmeat
$1/4$ cup dried bread crumbs
$1/4$ cup chopped fresh parsley
Juice and grated peel of 1 lemon
1 egg, beaten
$1/4$ cup heavy cream
Salt and freshly ground white pepper to taste

Preheat oven to 400° F. To make the stuffing: In a medium-sized bowl, combine all of the ingredients and mix together well.

Fill the prawns with the stuffing and place in a baking pan. Baste with the butter and bake for 4 to 5 minutes.

Place 4 stuffed prawns on each plate and spoon the *Vanilla Butter Cream Sauce* over the top. Garnish each serving with 1 fennel sprig and serve immediately.

YIELD: 4 SERVINGS

Vanilla Butter Cream Sauce

1 cup dry white wine
1 tablespoon pure vanilla extract

$1/4$ cup heavy cream
1 stick unsalted butter, cut into pieces

In a small saucepan, combine the wine and vanilla and heat on medium-high heat until reduced to $1/4$ cup. Reduce heat to simmer. Stir in the cream and simmer until begins to thicken. Remove from heat and whisk in the butter until smooth.

Wild Berry Cobbler with Lemon Curd Sauce

^{1}/$_2$ cup (1 stick) unsalted butter
1 cup all-purpose flour
1 ^{1}/$_4$ cups granulated sugar
1 teaspoon baking powder
^{1}/$_2$ cup heavy cream
2 cups mixed wild berries
1 recipe *Lemon Curd Sauce* (see recipe below)

Preheat oven to 350° F. In a 10-inch glass baking dish, melt the butter and set aside.

In a medium-sized bowl, mix together the flour, 1 cup of the sugar, and the baking powder. Stir in the cream and mix together well. Spoon the mixture over the reserved butter.

In a medium-sized saucepan, heat together the remaining sugar and the berries until just warm. Pour the berry mixture over the crust mixture and bake for 35 to 45 minutes, or until the crust is golden brown and rises to the surface. Let cool slightly on a wire rack. Cut into servings.

Ladle ^{1}/$_4$ cup *Lemon Curd Sauce* onto each plate and place 1 slice of the cobbler on the sauce. Top with more sauce and serve immediately.

YIELD: 8 SERVINGS

Lemon Curd Sauce

6 egg yolks, beaten
1 cup granulated sugar
1 cup fresh lemon juice
1 tablespoon grated lemon peel
2 sticks unsalted butter, cut into small pieces

Strain the egg yolks through a sieve into medium-sized heavy saucepan. Add the sugar, lemon juice, and lemon peel and stir together well. Cook on low heat, stirring constantly, until the mixture thickens enough to coat the back of a spoon.

Stir in the butter, 1 piece at a time, until fully blended. Continue to cook until the sauce again coats the back of a spoon.

Chapter 14

Creamy Eggs Rialto

Savory Strudel of Wild Mushrooms, Piñons,
Goat Cheese & Watercress

Fresh Fruits Romanoff

Vanilla Roll with Strawberries & Chocolate Buttercream

Apple Puffs with Cinnamon Syrup

Gingered Melon Ices with Berries

Eggs Bandito with Cilantro Hollandaise

Paonia Peach Ambrosia in Raspberry Puree

CHEF SANDY STRAUSS
The Lovelander Bed & Breakfast Inn, Loveland, Colorado

KELLI TREGEMBA

CHEF SANDY STRAUSS
The Lovelander
Bed & Breakfast Inn,
Loveland, Colorado

When our crews visited Loveland, Colorado, every person we met was a sheer delight. This quaint, little Victorian inn is managed by Sandy Strauss, and she is one of those rare personalities whose smile and genuine thoughtfulness somehow makes its way through the camera lens and into the hearts of the viewers. Sandy and her colleagues have developed an exceptionally loyal cadre of corporate and vacation travelers by doing what they do, very well.

Sandy is doing what hundreds of "Inn Country Chefs" and "Inn Country USA" fans wish they could do. Beginning with a Bachelor of Science degree in Secondary Language Arts from the University of Kansas and continuing through graduate studies in the world of academia, Sandy harbored a deep love for cookbooks and cooking. When she relocated from Kansas to Colorado in 1978 to concentrate on raising her two children, she began to discover an entirely new faculty of role models. From "The Frugal Gourmet" to "The Galloping Gourmet" and the best public television chefs in the business, Sandy began to develop and to master her own cooking techniques.

In 1988, Sandy joined Bob and Marilyn Wiltgen as manager of their Lovelander B & B Inn where she is equally at home greeting guests or preparing breakfast!

Creamy Eggs Rialto

8 eggs
$1/2$ cup milk
Pinch garlic powder
$1/4$ teaspoon onion powder
$1/2$ teaspoon salt
$1/4$ teaspoon freshly ground black pepper
Pinch Hungarian paprika
One 8-ounce package cream cheese, cut into $1/2$-inch cubes
1 scallion, chopped (include top)
3 fresh domestic mushrooms, cleaned, trimmed, and chopped
2 tablespoons chopped red bell peppers
2 canned whole mild green chilies, seeded and chopped

In a large bowl, beat the eggs, then stir in the milk and seasonings. Stir the cream cheese into the egg mixture, being careful not to break down the cubes. In a medium-sized bowl, mix together all of the vegetables.

Preheat oven to 350° F. Ladle $2/3$ cup of the egg mixture into each of 6 greased ramekins. Spoon 2 tablespoons of the vegetable mixture into each dish and stir gently to combine the mixtures.

Place the ramekins on a baking sheet and bake for 25 to 30 minutes, or until the eggs are set and puffed, gently stirring about halfway through the cooking time to keep the edges from cooking faster than the center. Serve immediately.

YIELD: 6 SERVINGS

Savory Strudel of Wild Mushrooms, Piñons, Goat Cheese & Watercress

2 ounces mixed dried wild mushrooms, well cleaned

Cream sherry

8 ounces fresh domestic mushrooms, cleaned and trimmed

2 tablespoons unsalted butter

2 tablespoons chopped red onions

Freshly ground black pepper to taste

1 teaspoon dried oregano

1 tablespoon sherry or to taste

1/2 cup toasted piñon nuts

1 puff pastry sheet, at room temperature

1 bunch fresh watercress, rinsed, trimmed, and dried

3 to 4 ounces goat cheese, crumbled

1 egg, slightly beaten

Ground paprika

Toasted piñon nuts

> There are some dishes that are equally at home regardless of the course or the time of day. Sandy's savory strudel of wild mushrooms, pine nuts, goat cheese, and watercress works well as an interesting breakfast side dish and is also a superb presentation at high tea.

In a shallow bowl, place the wild mushrooms and pour the sherry over all to nearly cover. Let stand for 30 minutes or until the dried mushrooms are rehydrated, checking occasionally to push the dried mushrooms into the sherry. Remove the mushrooms from the bowl and squeeze dry, reserving liquid for other uses. Trim off the woody stem ends and chop both the wild and domestic mushrooms.

In a large skillet, melt the butter and sauté all of the mushrooms to extract liquor. Stir in the next five ingredients and cook until the mushrooms are browned and well seasoned. Drain well and let cool.

Unfold the pastry sheet and roll or pat out into an 8 x 10-inch rectangle. Arrange half of the watercress in a single layer overlapping the ends to cover the pastry to within 1/2 inch of the edges. Sprinkle the cheese evenly over the watercress.

Spread the mushroom mixture over the cheese layer and press the filling slightly into the pastry to keep in place when rolling. Roll up the pastry from long end to long end. Pinch the seam and tuck the ends to seal the pastry.

Preheat oven to 400° F. Place the strudel seam-side down on an ungreased baking sheet, brush with the egg, and sprinkle with the paprika. Bake for 25 to 30 minutes or until puffed and golden. Remove and let stand for 20 minutes before slicing. Cut the strudel into 6 slices.

Divide the remaining watercress among the plates and place 1 slice of the strudel on the bed of watercress. Scatter the extra piñon nuts around each plate and serve immediately.

YIELD: 6 SERVINGS

Fresh Fruits Romanoff

Sour cream or plain yogurt
Fresh nectarines or peaches, rinsed, peeled, and sliced
Fresh ripe bananas, sliced diagonally
Fresh lemon juice
Fresh strawberries, rinsed, hulled, and sliced vertically
Fresh blueberries, rinsed
Fresh raspberries, rinsed
Brown sugar
Fresh mint leaves, rinsed

For a buffet, use a large, round flan dish or flat tray; for individual servings, use dessert plates or shallow dessert bowls with straight sides and flat bottoms.

Spread the bottom of the dish with a layer of the sour cream to even thickness, about $^1/_2$ inch deep. Drizzle the nectarines and bananas with the lemon juice and toss gently to prevent browning of fruit.

Arrange rows of fruit concentrically and/or diagonally using contrasts in color and variations in fruit size to create a visually interesting pattern on top of the cream base, leaving some small space for the white to show through. Sprinkle liberally with the sugar and chill for at least 20 minutes or until the sugar has dissolved into a brown glazing syrup. Garnish with the mint leaves and serve.

YIELD: VARIABLE SERVINGS

Vanilla Roll with Strawberries & Chocolate Buttercream

4 eggs, separated
$2/3$ cup granulated sugar
1 $1/2$ teaspoons pure vanilla extract
Pinch salt
$1/4$ teaspoon cream of tartar
$2/3$ cup cake flour
Confectioners' sugar
1 recipe *Chocolate Buttercream* (see recipe below)
Chocolate shavings
1 cup chopped fresh strawberries
Fresh strawberries, rinsed, hulled, and sliced vertically
Chocolate curls
Fresh mint leaves, rinsed

Grease and flour a 11 x 15-inch jelly-roll pan and line with parchment paper. Grease and flour again.

In a large bowl, slightly beat the egg yolks. Continue beating and slowly add $1/3$ cup of the granulated sugar until the batter reaches ribbon stage. Beat in the vanilla and set aside.

In a medium-sized bowl, beat the egg whites until foamy. Add the salt and cream of tartar and beat until soft peaks form. Slowly add the remaining granulated sugar and beat until stiff, glossy peaks form. Fold the flour into the reserved egg yolk mixture in stages. (Do not overmix.) Fold one-third of the stiff egg whites into the batter just to lighten, then gently fold in the remaining stiff egg whites until well combined.

Preheat oven to 350° F. Spread the batter in the prepared pan and bake for 10 to 15 minutes, or until the cake springs back when gently touched in the middle. (Do not overbake.) Let cool in the pan for 5 minutes.

Lay a kitchen towel on a work surface and cover with parchment paper and dust with the confectioners' sugar.

Carefully invert the cooled cake onto the paper-covered towel and remove the paper that has baked onto the cake. Carefully roll up the cake in the sugar-dusted paper liner (short end to short end for larger dessert pieces or long edge to long edge for smaller tea cakes). Wrap the rolled up cake with the kitchen towel and let cool completely on a wire rack.

Unroll the cake and spread the Chocolate Buttercream to within $1/2$ inch of the edge of the roll. Sprinkle the chocolate shavings over the filling and gently press in place. Sprinkle the chopped strawberries evenly over the filling and gently press in place. Carefully roll the cake jelly-roll style and chill before slicing.

Slice and garnish with the strawberry fans, chocolate curls, and mint leaves. Serve immediately.

YIELD: 8 SERVINGS OR 12 TO 14 TEA CAKES

Chocolate Buttercream

3 egg yolks
7 tablespoons granulated sugar
$1/3$ cup water
$3/4$ cup softened unsalted butter
$1/2$ cup whipping cream
1 teaspoon pure vanilla extract
1 cup shaved milk or dark chocolate

In a medium-sized bowl, beat the egg yolks until light yellow. Set aside.

In a heavy saucepan, combine the sugar and water and cook on medium heat, stirring constantly, until the sugar dissolves and the mixture comes to a boil. Continue to boil gently, without stirring, until the mixture reaches the soft ball stage (239° F on a candy thermometer), while brushing the crystallized sugar from the sides of the saucepan with a pastry brush dipped in cold water. Immediately remove from heat and pour over the reserved egg yolks, beating constantly while pouring. Continue beating until the mixture is light and fluffy. Set aside.

In a small bowl, cream the butter. Very gradually beat the butter, a little at a time, into the reserved egg yolk mixture and beat until smooth and shiny.

In another bowl, whip the cream and vanilla to full volume. Fold one-third of the whipped cream into the buttercream to lighten, then gradually fold in the remaining whipped cream and the chocolate.

Apple Puffs with Cinnamon Syrup

^{1}/$_4$ cup fresh lemon juice
^{1}/$_2$ teaspoon ground cinnamon
^{1}/$_2$ cup packed dark brown sugar
2 medium baking apples, peeled and very thinly sliced
4 eggs, beaten
^{3}/$_4$ cup whole milk
^{3}/$_4$ cup all-purpose flour
Dash ground nutmeg
Dash salt
^{1}/$_4$ cup (^{1}/$_2$ stick) unsalted butter, melted
Confectioners' sugar

In a deep bowl, mix together the lemon juice, cinnamon, and brown sugar. Toss the apple slices in the lemon juice mixture to coat. Set aside.

In a small bowl, combine the eggs and milk and blend thoroughly. In a medium-sized bowl, stir together the flour, nutmeg, and salt.

Spray the bottom and sides of 4 ramekins with Baker's Joy. Spoon 1 tablespoon of the butter into each dish. Divide *half* of the apple slices among the dishes, arranging the slices over the butter. Add the egg mixture to the flour mixture, stirring just to blend, and divide the mixture among the dishes.

Preheat oven to 425° F. Arrange the remaining apple slices in a spoke pattern on top of the batter. Place the ramekins on a baking sheet and bake for 20 to 30 minutes or until puffed and set.

In a small saucepan, heat the remaining lemon juice mixture just until bubbly and all of the brown sugar is dissolved. Remove the puffs from the oven and drizzle with the cinnamon syrup. Dust with the confectioners' sugar and serve immediately.

YIELD: 4 SERVINGS

Gingered Melon Ices with Berries

1 ¹/₂ tablespoons honey
1 teaspoon grated fresh gingerroot
1 teaspoon fresh lemon juice
1 ripe cantaloupe, rind removed and seeded
¹/₂ large ripe honeydew melon, rind removed and seeded
¹/₄ small seedless watermelon, rind removed and seeded
Fresh blueberries, rinsed
Fresh raspberries, rinsed
Fresh mint leaves, rinsed
Zest of ¹/₂ orange
Zest of ¹/₂ lime

In a small bowl, mix together the honey, ginger, and lemon juice. Cut each melon into small chunks and place into 3 separate bowls. Divide the honey mixture evenly among the bowls and toss to distribute evenly. Marinate for at least 2 hours to overnight.

In a blender or food processor, puree each melon and its marinade separately, then freeze each puree until firm.

Scoop some of each melon ice into each goblet and sprinkle with the blueberries and raspberries. Garnish with the mint leaves and the orange and lime zest and serve immediately.

YIELD: 4 TO 6 SERVINGS

Eggs Bandito with Cilantro Hollandaise

Canola oil
12 flour tortillas, cut into $^1/_2$ x 4-inch
  thin strips
Ground cumin
$^1/_4$ teaspoon garlic powder
2 teaspoons fresh lime juice
3 ripe avocados, chopped
3 fresh Anaheim chili peppers, seeded
  and sliced
3 medium fresh tomatoes, chopped

3 large cloves garlic, finely chopped
6 scallions, chopped (include tops)
1 cup canned black beans, drained
  and well rinsed
1 cup cooked fresh corn
6 eggs, poached
1 recipe *Cilantro Hollandaise* (see
  recipe below)
Fresh cilantro, chopped

In a large skillet, heat at least 2 inches of the oil and fry the tortilla strips until crispy and golden. Drain on paper towels. Dust lightly with the cumin and set aside.

In a small bowl, mix together the garlic powder and lime juice and toss with the avocados. Set aside.

Arrange the reserved fried tortilla strips into a crisscrossed mound on each plate. Sprinkle the chili peppers, tomatoes, reserved avocados, garlic, scallions, beans, and corn over the tortilla strips (reserve some chili pepper slices and tomatoes). Top with 1 poached egg. Ladle $^1/_3$ cup *Cilantro Hollandaise* over each egg and top with the reserved chili pepper slices and tomatoes. Garnish with the cilantro and serve immediately.

YIELD: 6 SERVINGS

Since The Lovelander is a bed & breakfast, the concentration here is definitely the morning meal. Sandy has developed a variety of interesting egg dishes that differ from the usual morning fare at other inns. She admits proudly that she is not shy about the use of hollandaise in many of her dishes. "It adds a festive, almost celebratory touch," she explains, "and our guests appreciate the little bit of extra trouble that goes into the hollandaise." She's right. Here's proof!

Cilantro Hollandaise

4 egg yolks
3 tablespoons fresh lime juice
$^1/_2$ cup (1 stick) butter, divided
1 $^1/_2$ tablespoons finely chopped fresh cilantro

In a small saucepan, whisk together the egg yolks and lime juice on very low heat. Add $^1/_4$ cup of the butter and stir constantly until melted.

Add the remaining butter and the cilantro, stirring constantly, until the butter is melted and the sauce thickens. Makes 2 cups.

Paonia Peach Ambrosia in Raspberry Puree

One 10-ounce package frozen raspberries, thawed
$^1/_2$ cup chopped dried dates
$^1/_2$ cup lightly toasted fresh coconut
$^3/_4$ cup crushed *Victorian Vinegar Cookies* (see recipe below)
$^1/_4$ cup chopped pecans
$^1/_4$ cup fresh orange juice
$^1/_4$ teaspoon pure almond extract
1 teaspoon sherry
3 fresh peaches, peeled, halved, and pits removed
$^1/_2$ cup cold heavy cream
Fresh mint leaves, rinsed

In a blender or food processor, puree the raspberries. Strain to remove seeds and chill. In a food processor, combine the next four ingredients and pulse until just chunky and holds together. Set aside.

Preheat oven to 350° F. In a small bowl, blend together the orange juice, almond extract, and sherry and pour into a baking pan. Place the peaches cut-side up in the baking pan and mound the cookie filling in each peach center. Spoon the pan liquid over the peaches and bake, covered, for 15 to 20 minutes or until tender.

Spoon the chilled raspberry puree onto each plate. With a dropper or spoon, drip the cold cream around the edge of the raspberry pool, spacing drops evenly. Draw a toothpick through the centers of the cream drops to form a ring of hearts. Place 1 stuffed peach half in the center of each raspberry pool. Garnish with the mint leaves and serve immediately.

YIELD: 6 SERVINGS

Victorian Vinegar Cookies

$^1/_4$ cup ($^1/_2$ stick) softened butter
$^1/_4$ cup ($^1/_2$ stick) softened margarine
6 tablespoons granulated sugar
$^1/_2$ tablespoon white vinegar
$^3/_4$ cup plus 2 tablespoons all-purpose flour
$^1/_4$ teaspoon baking soda
$^1/_2$ cup finely chopped walnuts

Preheat oven to 300° F. In a medium-sized bowl, cream the butter and margarine until light. Add the sugar and vinegar and beat until fluffy. Sift in the flour and baking soda and stir until evenly blended. (Do not overwork the dough.) Stir in the walnuts and mix together well.

Drop by teaspoonsful onto an ungreased baking sheet and bake for 20 to 30 minutes or until lightly golden. Let cool on parchment paper. Makes 3 dozen.

Appendix

If you have enjoyed this unique collection of recipes from chefs and their inns, we encourage you write or call the inns with your thoughts and comments. Even better, visit the inns and get to know these gracious and friendly people.

Carter House/Hotel Carter
301 L St.
Eureka, CA 95501
tel: 707-444-8062; 800-404-1390
fax: 707-444-8067
Mark & Christi Carter, Innkeepers
Jean-Louis Hamiche, Chef

Clifton—The Country Inn
1296 Clifton Inn Dr.
Charlottesville, VA 22901
tel: 804-971-1800
fax: 804-971-7098
Craig & Donna Hartman, Innkeepers
Craig Hartman, Chef

The Fearrington House ❖
2000 Fearrington, Village Center
Pittsboro, NC 27312
tel: 919-542-2121
fax: 919-542-4202
R.B. Fitch, Owner
Richard Delany, General Manager
Cory Mattson, Chef

The Governor's Inn ❖
86 Main St.
Ludlow, VT 05149
tel: 802-228-8830; 800-468-3766
fax: 802-228-7288
Charlie & Deedy Marble, Innkeepers
Deedy Marble, Chef

Grant Corner Inn
122 Grant Ave.
Santa Fe, NM 87501
tel: 505-983-6678
fax: 505-983-1526
Louise Stewart, Chef and Innkeeper
Pat Walter, Chef

Greyfield Inn
(Cumberland Island, GA)
PO Box 900
Fernandina Beach, FL 32035-0900
tel: 904-261-6408; 912-267-0180
fax: 904-321-0666
Mitty & Mary Jo Ferguson, Innkeepers
Shelley Walker, Chef

The Homestead Inn
420 Field Point Rd.
Greenwich, CT 06830
tel/fax: 203-869-7500
Lessie Davison & Nancy Smith,
   Innkeepers
Jacques Thiebeult, Chef

Inn at Blackberry Farm
1471 W. Millers Cove Rd.
Walland, TN 37886
tel: 423-984-8166; 800-862-7610 (res.)
fax: 423-983-5708
Kreis B. & Sandy Beall, Owners
Barry Marshall, Innkeeper
John Fleer, Chef

❖ *Designates inns that have their own cookbooks.*

Josephine's Bed & Breakfast
PO Box 4767
Seaside, FL 32459
tel: 904-231-1940; 800-848-1840
fax: 904-231-1791
Jody, Judy & Bruce Albert & Sean
Herbert, Innkeepers
Bruce & Jody Albert, Chefs
Doug Alley, Chef

The Lords Proprietors' Inn ❖
300 N. Broad St.
Edenton, NC 27932
tel: 919-482-3641
fax: 919-482-2432
Arch & Jane Edwards, Innkeepers
Kevin Yokley, Chef

The Lovelander
 Bed & Breakfast Inn
217 W. 4th St.
Loveland, CO 80537
tel: 970-669-0798; 800-459-6694
fax: 970-669-0797
Marilyn & Bob Wiltgen, Innkeepers
Sandy Strauss, Chef

Prospect Hill Plantation Inn
Rt. 3 (Hwy. 613), Box 430
Trevilians, VA 23093
tel: 540-967-0844; 800-277-0844
fax: 540-967-0102
Michael & Laura Sheehan, Innkeepers
Michael Sheehan, Chef

Richmond Hill Inn
87 Richmond Hill Dr.
Asheville, NC 28806
tel: 704-252-7313
fax: 704-252-8726
Susan Michel, Innkeeper
Lucy Hamilton, Consulting Chef

Rose Inn
PO Box 6576, Rt. 34 N.
Ithaca, NY 14851-6576
tel: 607-533-7905
fax: 607-533-7908
Charles & Sherry Rosemann, Innkeepers
Sherry Rosemann, Chef

Recipes Arranged by Chef/Inn

Index

V

About the Author

C. Vincent Shortt is the founder and President of Shortt Stories Teleproductions, Inc., based in Winston-Salem, North Carolina. He has been a leading force in the hospitality industry and an award-winning producer of film and television programming for the past 20 years. He is an acknowledged authority on the food and beverage industry and a contributing editor and guest columnist for a variety of hospitality industry publications. Mr. Shortt is the only four-time recipient of the Pepsi MVP Award in the United States and has been honored by the National Restaurant Association with bronze, silver, and gold awards for menu design excellence.

Mr. Shortt is the executive producer of the television series "Inn Country USA," "Historic Hotels of America," "Inn Country Chefs," and many other highly acclaimed film and video documentaries airing on public television, the Travel Channel, and a variety of other cable television venues. He is the author of the revised edition of *How to Open and Successfully Operate a Country Inn*, plus *The Innkeepers Collection Cookbook* and *The Inn Country USA Cookbook*, companion cookbooks to his TV series "Inn Country USA," all published by Berkshire House Publishers, Lee, Massachusetts. He and his wife, Ann, live in Advance, North Carolina.

Mr. Shortt can be reached on the World Wide Web through http://www.travelchannel.com or by e-mail at inntv@aol.com.